Yellowstone Park

Yellowstone Park

Bruce Staples

Frank
Amato

PORTLAND

River Journal

Volume 4, Number 1, 1996

Bruce Staples lives in Idaho Falls, Idaho and has fished Yellowstone Park waters for nearly thirty years. He is the author of *"Snake River Country Flies and Waters"* (Frank Amato Publications, 1992) and has contributed articles to *American Angler* and *Fly Tyer*, *Fly Fishing* and *Fly Fisher* magazines. He writes a monthly column for the Idaho Falls *Post Register*, enjoys and instructs all levels of fly tying and contributes to the preservation of the east Idaho environment. He is active in the Federation of Fly Fishers and is a long time member of the Upper Snake River Chapter (Snake River Cutthroats) of Trout Unlimited of Idaho Falls and the Upper Snake River Fly Fishers of Rexburg, Idaho.

◆

Acknowledgments

I express appreciation for help or information from Dan Carty of the U. S. Fish and Wildlife Agency in Yellowstone National Park; Bob Gresswell, formerly of the same agency; Terry Todd, engineer and pilot extraordinaire, and my wife Carol who knows best where to find me on Yellowstone Park Waters.

◆

Series Editor: Frank Amato

Subscriptions:
Softbound: $35.00 for one year (four issues)
$65.00 for two years
Hardbound Limited Editions: $95.00 one year, $170.00 for two years
Frank Amato Publications, Inc. • P.O. Box 82112 • Portland, Oregon 97282 • (503) 653-8108

Design: Alan Reid
Photography: Bruce Staples, Bob Trowbridge, Rich Tillotson and Kenneth Retallic
Map: Alan Reid
Printed in Hong Kong
Softbound ISBN:1-57188-044-5, Hardbound ISBN:1-57188-058-5
(Hardbound Edition Limited to 500 Copies)

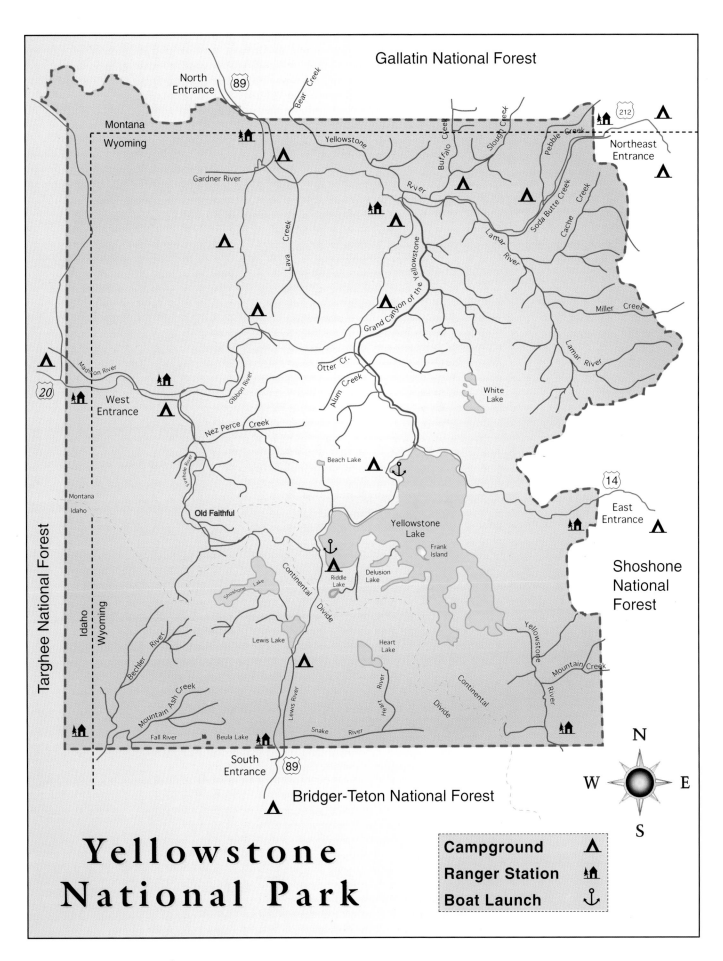

Yellowstone
National Park

Campground	▲
Ranger Station	▲▲
Boat Launch	⚓

Yellowstone Park

◆

The waters of Yellowstone National Park are the best inland trout habitat in our country, and this is extendible to saying that they are among the world's best. Nearly everything required for ideal trout residence has been preserved here by the national park concept: near perfect water quality, healthy riparian zones, good food production and ample spawning and habitation conditions.

Native Americans revered the area in which the Park is sited, and the first non–natives did little to desecrate it. Persons seeking sport or commercial gain came after the explorers, trappers and soldiers, and it was with them that misuse and misconceptions had the first serious impacts on fisheries. Until the late nineteenth century the salmonid population consisted of Montana grayling, mountain whitefish and three subspecies of cutthroat trout: Snake River fine spotted, west slope and Yellowstone. Another misuse came, some argue, when exotic salmonids; brown trout, brook trout and lake trout were introduced into Park waters in the late nineteenth century. It is hard to deny this because only a remnant of grayling remain and cutthroat populations are diminished. In the first half of the twentieth century other introductions were made, but only the rainbow trout succeeded. The result of the native species and those introduced is the current stock of trout in Park waters.

Exploitation of Yellowstone National Park fisheries went on for decades. So did miscomprehension by managers. Fish in huge numbers were squandered by anglers as permissible bag limits and inadequate enforcement encouraged waste. Commercial fishing decimated populations. Genetic stocks were scrambled in hatchery operations and by introductions across watersheds. By midcentury Yellowstone Park fisheries were headed for collapse, and it was realized that only strict measures would restore former trout and grayling populations. Continuous reduction of daily bag limits on exotic trout and essentially catch and release for native species and their hybrids has helped. So has closure of sections of waters for spawning and habitat protection. Likewise, restriction of terminal gear has aided in salmonid survival. The use of lead weight was banned a few years ago, and in 1994 a fee ($10 per season, $5 per week) was established for a Park angling license with funds acquired earmarked for law enforcement, fisheries studies and habitat preservation.

Enlightened management is close to minimizing misuse of Park fisheries, so the future looks bright for resident salmonids. Misconceptions remain. Perhaps the biggest is that the Park was always "full of trout". Up to about 1889 many Park waters were barren.

All Park waters host trout very near their holding capacity, a tribute to quality, but another misconception is that Park waters are rich in basic nutrients required to build a broad and varied food chain. This is false, regardless of numerous works

Quality water: Slough Creek in meadows below the campground.

◆

claiming it is the case, because nearly all the Park is underlain by notoriously insolvent volcanic rhyolites. Thermal features, common contributors to Park surface waters, supply nutrients, but not necessarily the calcium bicarbonate needed to build organic structures. Why, then, are good numbers of salmonids with large individuals present in Park waters? Simply because all other aspects needed are present. The best work addressing habitat, condition and history of Yellowstone Park fisheries is the book "Freshwater Wilderness: Yellowstone Fish and Their World" by John Varley and Paul Schullery. All anglers who appreciate Yellowstone Park waters should read this work. Meanwhile the scope of this book is to reveal Yellowstone Park waters, heralded and not so well known, in the general sense. Let's take a look at these waters which are among the very best on the face of this earth for trout.

Snake River Drainage

The Snake River drainage contains a larger variety of waters than any of those in the Park. Three of the Park's major lakes (Heart, Lewis and Shoshone) are here as are three of its larger rivers (Heart, Lewis and Snake). The brown trout population of the drainage within the Park exceeds that of all other Park drainages combined. To the east on Two Ocean Plateau is a possible passage site of the past where cutthroat trout moved from the Pacific drainage to the Atlantic drainage. This is Two

Ocean Creek, just south of the Park, which splits on the Continental Divide to flow to either drainage. Besides the major waters, prime small waters including Crawfish Creek, Moose Creek, Outlet Creek, Pocket Lake, Polecat Creek, and Shoshone Creek grace the drainage and offer near solitude.

Snake River

The Snake River begins just south of Yellowstone National Park and drains the west slope of the Two Ocean Plateau. After entering the Park, it runs northwesterly while dropping almost one thousand feet in ten miles. It slows in a large sloping meadow as it approaches its confluence with Heart River. Here it arcs around Big Game Ridge to flow southerly to a canyon with deep pools, swift runs and rapids holding good cutthroat trout. After exiting the canyon below the Heart River confluence, the Snake River flows in a broad westerly arc more frequently visited by anglers and sightseers. This country is accessed from the South Entrance Ranger Station, near which the river is usually forded. The Snake River is a major runoff stream, and its season depends on snowfall and spring weather. Normally, it becomes fishable by mid-July. The river, the trunk of the Park's third largest drainage, experiences some natural siltation, but remains an excellent fishery. Whitefish make up at least half of the resident salmonids, but are a credible sportfish. They take small dry and wet flies, fight well, but not enduringly like coin-habitant cutthroat trout. Pools are the best holding water, and little cover other than boulders and sweepers is present. Riffles and runs hold mayflies with *Baetis* (blue winged olive) and *Epeorus* (slate-cream dun) species being most numerous. Rhyacophila caddis are abundant, and a representation of giant stoneflies is present.

Two species of char, as well as trout, inhabit the Snake River. Rare lake and brook trout are swept down through Lewis River from Lewis Lake above. In the autumn, they also appear to follow brown trout spawning out of Jackson Lake. Lake trout may also wander out of Heart Lake, down through Heart River and into the Snake River. Brown trout, like brook trout and lake trout originate from late nineteenth century plants in Lewis and Shoshone lakes. In terms of use for the fly fisher, brown trout have been most successful. They have made widespread migrations downstream as far as Jackson Lake. They and brook trout have spread into tributaries such as Polecat Creek. They also grow to large sizes.

I fish these waters around Labor Day, and success comes by presenting terrestrial patterns. Good trout can be found up to Snake Hot Springs, but to go beyond is to expend time in walking or riding rather than enjoying the better downstream fishing. Blue winged olive (*Baetis*) and slate–cream dun mayflies and caddisflies can also be found on the stream during these days. With nymphs, emergers and adults of these you will catch whitefish, but they can reach over twenty inches and are therefore respectable opponents. So are horseflies which frequent the meadows, but they are the reason why a size twelve humpy is a good pattern for the area.

Two subspecies of cutthroat trout are native to the Snake River. These are the more numerous Yellowstone subspecies and the rarer Snake River fine spotted subspecies. Both are powerful fighters and elegant to behold. With little overhead shelter from forests, cliffs or overhangs, trout here do not linger in open waters during direct sunlight. Thus mornings and evenings are the best times to fish here during midsummer. Earlier in the year as runoff ebbs, leech patterns, which imitate earthworms, or large stonefly nymph patterns are effective. A bit later, one can also take trout on large adult stonefly patterns during the brief emergence. Wading is difficult early in the season because of the mainly rubble bottom and swiftness of the water. This makes August into October the most pleasant time to fish the Snake River. One must watch the weather to avoid chilling storms and slick roads late in the season, but bluebird days can be numerous with brown and cutthroat trout responding to terrestrial, floating caddis and mayfly patterns. Then, as time advances into October brown trout from Jackson Lake move through on their spawning run. I fish this run which is smaller than most other Park brown trout runs. It is thus difficult to identify in time, so I have left my home in east Idaho before sunup to encounter these browns, travelled north through the length of Jackson Hole to Yellowstone's south

◆

Yellowstone's sole native trout: the cutthroat.

Lewis Falls, Lewis River.

◆

"The Channel". Thus, I discuss it in relation to Shoshone Lake, but immediately below Lewis Lake, is a reach fo the Lewis river that has excellent cover for trout, so that in the summer well placed terrestrial patterns bring strikes. Riffles provide aquatic insects, and from mid–June through September caddis, blue winged olive and pale morning dun patterns will bring action. But the major angling attraction here is the run of brown trout that migrates out of Lewis Lake beginning in late September. These hit best on streamer and nymph patterns. Below Lewis Falls is what Charlie Brooks considered to be the most puzzling trout stream he knew. About the end of June, depending on runoff conditions, there occurs, like on "The Channel", a green drake emergence. Large browns respond to this, but timing is critical. Before this emergence, however, I have experienced some unusual, but not unique angling in this meadow as stone-flies emerging in the canyon below are carried by the wind to the meadow. I have also found through a few evening experiences that the large browns can be fooled by a hair mouse offered over select cover. After this meadow reach, Lewis River drops rapidly into a steep canyon surpassed in the Park in depth, length and beauty only by the Grand and Black canyons of the Yellowstone River. This section of river, however, is of little interest to the angler because it is nearly devoid of holding water and therefore holds small trout.

As with several other rivers in Yellowstone National Park, the Lewis was once mainly barren of trout. All these streams and their tributaries were stocked with combinations of brook, brown, cutthroat and rainbow trout beginning just before the

◆

Moose Falls on Crawfish Creek.

entrance, a distance of one hundred and fifty miles only to find that I am a week late. Then there have been years when I have arrived at about the same time as the brown trout, and a day of twenty to thirty trout caught and released has resulted. These, of course, will be mostly browns, but included are a few cut-throat and lake trout. These days are unforgettable, but during them or on the forgettable days angling is done with an eye on the sky as late autumn blizzards are possible. Several times I have left with snowflakes swirling while I make haste to leave before the highway to Jackson becomes treacherous. Some times in the past I have made it to the south entrance by tra-versing the Ashton–Flagg Ranch Road. During some of these trips storms have moved in to make return by that road impos-sible. The result is the longer trip down to Jackson Hole. Then, after dinner in one of Jackson's fine restaurants and a visit with one of my angling friends, it is down the Snake River Canyon to home. So this short lived brown trout run signals the sea-son's end as inclement weather dominates at the end of October. The browns retire to Jackson Lake. The lake, in turn, wraps in ice and snow. Back upstream the Snake River cools, so resident cutthroat trout wait out winter for their turn to per-form duty to sustain their kind.

Lewis River

Of Park rivers the Lewis alone flows from one major lake (Shoshone Lake) and through another (Lewis Lake). So differ-ent is Lewis River between Shoshone and Lewis lakes from the rest of its reach that anglers call it Lewis River Channel, or turn of the century. Brown trout now dominate the Lewis River except in one location, the reach between Lewis River Canyon and the Snake River confluence. In this beautiful reach of river native cutthroat trout share the stream with brown trout.

Lewis Lake

Lewis Lake is more approachable and therefore more heavily fished than Shoshone. These facts are not reasons for writing it off, for Lewis Lake contains an excellent population of brown trout and lake trout. Trout here may not rival those in Shoshone Lake in to numbers but they do in size, particularly the lake trout which have individuals exceeding thirty pounds. With respect to lake trout, Lewis Lake is a refuge. Its original stock came from Lake Michigan in the late nineteenth century. From its now excellent population comes the genetic material to reestablish Lake Michigan's lake trout population. So far, attempts to do so with fry and fingerlings have not been entirely successful because of major deterioration in Lake Michigan's water quality.

Most of the Lewis Lake east shoreline is skirted by the South Entrance–West Thumb Highway. Thus, this shoreline is accessible to wading and float tubing anglers who take brown or lake trout by presenting leech or streamer patterns on sinking or sink–tip lines regardless of weather conditions. Winds commonly limit summertime angling to early morning and evening hours for those presenting speckled dun and midge imitations. Wind and waves also make Lewis Lake, like

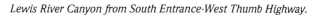

Lewis River Canyon from South Entrance-West Thumb Highway.

Lewis River between Lewis and Shoshone lakes.

Shoshone and Yellowstone lakes, extremely dangerous. Less than fifty degrees Fahrenheit are common summertime temperatures in these lakes, and boaters have perished over the years from hypothermia or drowned in each. For the cautious and prepared boater destinations across Lewis Lake are worth approaching. Perhaps the best is the northwest corner of the lake around submerged hot springs and the inlet of Lewis River Channel. This area can also be approached by the Lewis Lake–Lewis River Channel trail from north of Lewis Lake. The water at the inlet and adjacent hot spring area is also fished effectively from a float tube backpacked to this location. Just off the South Entrance–West Thumb Highway at the south end of Lewis Lake is the popular campground and boat dock from which boaters embark to fish Lewis Lake or cross to the Lewis River Channel and Shoshone Lake. The campground is an ideal base from which to wade the shoreline. Cruising brown trout will be the most common quarry, and during wind free mornings and evenings fishing for them can be exhilarating. If one wants a crack at lake trout, a good early and late season strategy is to embark in a float tube along the shoreline where rocky bottoms abound. I relish wading the shoreline on September and October evenings immersed in the cold, pure high country air that refreshes body and soul. Casting streamers is a rewarding experience, but migrating ducks and geese passing overhead and coyotes wailing their presence in the thick jackpine forest makes being here a privilege. The sun sets and the air temperature plummets making one anticipate the sleeping bag and hot beverage awaiting in Lewis Lake Campground.

Lewis River Channel and Shoshone Lake

Shoshone Lake is the second largest lake in Yellowstone National Park. This beautiful lake of about twelve square miles in surface area, nestles in a bulge of the Continental Divide. It is also the largest lake not touched by a road in the conterminous United States of America! Development by man here is the ranger stations at the outlet, on Windy Point halfway down the north shore and a system of primitive campsites. Backpackers reach the lake from Old Faithful, Bechler Ranger

West end of Shoshone Lake and Shoshone Geyser Basin.

Station, Norris Pass and trailheads above Lewis Lake. By far the most attractive access for the angler is to traverse northwest across Lewis Lake, by canoe or boat from the campground, to the mouth of Lewis River Channel. As the east shore slips away it is as if one goes back about one hundred years. The swish of the canoe paddles mesmerize thoughts to times when only those from the nearby communities experienced the fisheries in the Lewis River system. Before 1890 these waters were barren because of Lewis Falls below Lewis Lake, but everything required to sustain salmonid was present. True, the chemistry of the system was lean because of the insoluble rhyolitic country rock, but aquatic insects, mollusks, crustaceans and annelids were and remain present in quantity. Terrestrial insects thrived on the lake and stream shores. Then in 1890 fingerling Loch Leven brown trout from hatcheries in the eastern states were released in Shoshone and Lewis Lake. In the same year, lake trout from Lake Michigan were released in both lakes. Later, brook trout were released. The result was spectacular. Brown trout grew to several pounds, brook trout to about three pounds and lake trout in excess of thirty pounds. Brook trout are caught less frequently than in the past, perhaps in part because Pocket Lake, from which they were chemically eradicated in the 1970s (they remain in Moose Creek and the headwaters of Shoshone Creek), now contains the Heart Lake strain of cutthroat trout. Cutthroat moving out of Pocket Lake are now caught in Shoshone Lake.

Shoshone Lake is at nearly 8,000 feet elevation. Thus, time was required before trout could occupy Shoshone Lake. By the 1920s, however, commercial fisheries were sited on Shoshone Lake (and Lewis and Yellowstone lakes) to provide table fare for Park hotels. Anglers got the idea to fish Shoshone Lake after being served this table fare, and "anything goes" was the rule. Huge numbers of trout were wasted, and the lake became impacted by the effects of motorized boats, discarded garbage and the seepage of human wastes. In 1961 power boats were excluded from Shoshone Lake, Heart Lake, parts of Yellowstone Lake and Lewis Lake. Efforts to restore power boating to Lewis Lake were successful later, but Shoshone Lake (and Heart Lake) remains free of pollution from this source. So strict are efforts to minimize pollution of this high quality water that persons leaving the lake without garbage are viewed suspiciously by rangers, and woe to the individual who leaves a messy camp or is observed discarding waste to the lake.

Shoshone Lake holds excellent angling if one follows a seasonal game plan. It goes like this. Ice out occurs about the first of June. Trout are usually quite active through June, particularly

Twenty-Six inch brown being released in Shoshone Lake.

around submerged weed beds which host fresh water shrimp, snails and aquatic insects. All of this means one must either carry float tubes or traverse the Lewis River Channel. Canoeing or boating (the use of motorized boats is also prohibited on the Channel above Lewis Lake) is most practical because it permits convenient access to the entire lake. As June progresses, a prolific midge emergence brings brown trout to the surface on calm mornings and evenings. Floating lines with long leaders apply, and hookups provide the most exciting fly fishing that Shoshone Lake offers. Overlapping the midge emergence, a speckled dun emergence occurs from Shoshone Lake, and trout respond in the same manner as they do to midges. A little known and very localized emergence also takes place in the latter half of June, that of large stoneflies in the upper reach of Lewis River Channel. Some of the adults produced are blown onto the outlet bay, so adult stonefly imitations will attract cruising brown trout.

After June, Shoshone Lake warms, and most fish seek cool, deep waters. This reduces angling success significantly, so I recommend that you investigate other water from after the Fourth of July to around Labor Day. As the countryside cools in September, return to Shoshone Lake, but with a different approach. Now, brown trout migrate toward the outlet bay to enter Lewis River Channel to spawn. Large colorful streamers and sinking or sink–tip lines are required at these times. So is a stout constitution as the bluebird days of late September and early October can be punctuated by the first autumn snows and temperatures that can plunge to below zero degrees Fahrenheit. So what Shoshone Lake lacks with respect to con-

Trail Sign on Pitchstone Plateau.

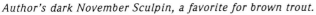

Author's dark November Sculpin, a favorite for brown trout.

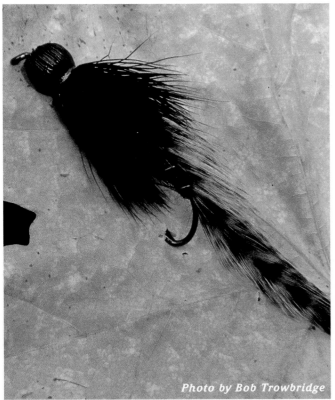

Photo by Bob Trowbridge

venience it compensates for in seasonal angling, the key to enjoying its fine fishery. But even if one does not experience the quality angling here, a visit to this lake, the largest undeveloped body of water in the lower forty–eight states, is worth the trip to grasp the extent of what remains of high quality water in our country.

The autumn brown trout run is only one aspect of fishing Lewis River Channel. Throughout spring and summer it offers excellent fishing for brown and lake trout.

In spring my companions and I enjoy excellent angling during our traverse to Shoshone Lake. The first mile of the Channel to the "Point of Rocks" Pool is really an extension of Lewis Lake. Canoes are ideal for fishing these waters. Float tubes packed in from the trailhead north of Lewis Lake are also appropriate, but do not permit the angler to investigate as much water. Just above "Point of Rocks" begins the meadow through which most of the Channel flows. In the early season streamers cast into the holes such as near "Harvey's Point" bring strikes from powerful, enduring browns. Late in the spring, a green drake emergence occurs here, so the same browns and an occasional lake trout can be taken on the surface. Pale morning dun and blue winged olive mayflies are also present here, but by the end of July terrestrial insects become more important. As the name "Aquarium Pool" suggests, the waters here are clear enough so that cruising fish are easily seen coming to the fly, whether wet or dry.

Except for the extreme lower end, most of this meadow reach is easily waded. The rapids above the meadows are easily

Twenty-two inch cutthroat from Beaver Creek.

Heart Lake Drainage

Tucked away in the east lap of Mount Sheridan and just over the Continental Divide from Yellowstone Lake is the most pristine large fishery in Yellowstone National Park. This is the Heart Lake drainage, a treasure by any standard. If you walk the four and a half miles from the Heart Lake trailhead on the South Entrance–West Thumb highway to the top of Paycheck Pass, Heart Lake Basin will be within your view. At ones feet, the apex of Heart Lake Geyser Basin courses to the northwest corner of Heart Lake which sparkles like a sapphire in the morning breeze. To the left is the Continental Divide. In the distance beyond, the Absaroka Range guards the east boundary of the Park. In the middle distance where Beaver Creek flows to the lake is the long, mysterious peninsula which nearly crosses the lake to divide the outlet bay from Heart Lake proper. Beyond in the lodgepole forest are the traces of Surprise Creek and Outlet Creek, which combine to flow into Heart River just below the lake. The trace of Heart River marks the outlet of the basin which contributes waters to the Snake River. To the right the rocky dome of Mount Sheridan dominates the scene. Snowfields garland its heights and supply melt waters to the basin. Peculiarly, the eastern flank of Sheridan appears to slide into Heart Lake, the effect of faults which produce springs flowing to the lake.

In this drainage the only alteration is a network of trails, primitive campgrounds and the picturesque ranger station at the northwest corner of the lake. Backpackers, sightseers, anglers, photographers and horsemen travel the eight mile dis-

fished, but not rich with fish during summer. They become sated with browns after the terrestrial season wanes around Labor Day. Then the most spectacular angling on the Channel begins as brown trout in the lakes above and below migrate to its riffles to commence spawning that will continue well past the closing of angling season.

Heart Lake Basin holds prime grizzly bear habitat.

Photo by Ken Retallic

Lake trout go to double figure poundage in Heart Lake.

◆

tance from trailhead to ranger station from July through September. Up until 1960 the four and a half mile section from the trailhead to Paycheck Pass was a primitive road. Anglers portaged boats or canoes from the pass to the lake, a drop of five hundred feet in three miles. In 1960 the road was closed to all but foot and horseback travel.

Heart Lake and its tributaries are richer in dissolved nutrients than the other oligotrophic lake systems in the Park. Whether this is the reason for a larger variety of resident fish in the Heart Lake system than other Park waters is vague. At least nine of the 18 species of fish living in the Park are found in the Heart Lake system. Like the Yellowstone drainage to the north, Heart Lake Basin was not devoid of trout in historic times. Heart Lake historically hosted the Snake River cutthroat. The Yellowstone cutthroat is also native to Heart Lake, perhaps coming over Two Ocean Plateau via Two Ocean Creek and down the Snake River eons ago. All cutthroat are spring spawners, so the present cutthroats are probably crosses of the two subspecies. Whatever their origin, cutthroats of Heart Lake Basin are a wonderful sport fish. Excepting that they roll on the surface rather than jumping, their fight is like that of brown trout. Specimens here, in the outlet immediately below the lake and occasionally in Beaver Creek range upwards to eight pounds. These fish are protected by a catch and release regulation which helps ensure their presence for future generations.

The other sport fish in Heart Lake (whitefish are also present, but not commonly caught) is the lake trout. These were introduced at the same time as those into Lewis and Shoshone lakes. Lake trout are the biggest fish in Yellowstone National Park, and in depths of Heart Lake they reach their largest. In 1931 a 42–pound individual was taken here, and specimens between ten and thirty pounds are still common.

So what is a strategy for fishing Heart Lake Basin? The most enjoyable times for me were early June when groups of at least four were allowed to backpack into the Basin. We spent days enjoying the magnificent cutthroat which could be caught from the lakeshore, the outlet river and tributaries. Beaver Creek was a particular joy to fish where run–up cutthroat and lake trout foraged for sucker spawn. I lost many trout when

they were hooked and ran headlong down that beautiful meadow stream for the lake below. One could also catch cutthroat and lake trout from shore using large streamer and leech patterns. We would also test the beautiful Heart River. The first quarter mile of which winds slow with deep holes and runs. At this time, cutthroats had finished spawning and were ravenous. Any wet fly would fool them, but taking them with floating pale morning dun or caddis patterns was most exciting. Below this section a quarter mile of riffle and run water announces the canyon beginning at the Outlet Creek confluence, so fish in another water type could be enjoyed. Heart Lake Basin is prime grizzly bear habitat, and in order to protect them, the Basin was closed in 1986 to human incursion during the month of June. I cannot forget those days in June in the Basin where I encountered the best angling I have experienced in the Park. I also cannot forget the huge grizzly bear tracks that obliterated all footprints on the trail to Heart River.

With warming and lowering of water in July, trout migrate into Heart Lake from the outlet and tributary streams. The exceptions are cutthroat trout in the upper reaches of Heart River which will partake of an excellent stonefly emergence that begins in the canyon below Outlet Creek. Also, if one fishes the lake littorals in early and late daylight, good angling for cruising trout awaits. Wading or tubing the shoreline is comfortable because the shallow portions warm to above 60 degrees Fahrenheit. Angling alternatives include the hike up Outlet Creek to Outlet Lake to sample a population of small, eager cutthroat. There is also the hike down the Heart River which for about three miles cuts a brawling canyon, then tran-

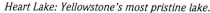

Heart Lake: Yellowstone's most pristine lake.

Sand hill cranes are common residents of Yellowstone's meadowlands.

scends a beautiful meadow to meet the Snake River.

One of the best ways to encounter large lake trout in Heart Lake is to fish the shore just east of the ranger station in mid-September. At this time lake trout come to the rocky shoreline to spawn. By wading or float tubing one can present streamers to lake trout and the cutthroat that follow them. As time advances, inclement weather reaches Heart Lake Basin, so for the prudent angler the season ends before October storms drop snows which endanger the hike to the basin.

At the end of one June trip we left camp on the outlet bay accompanied by leaden skies and a cold rain. Gone were the memories of glissading the slope of Mount Sheridan two days

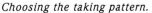

Choosing the taking pattern.

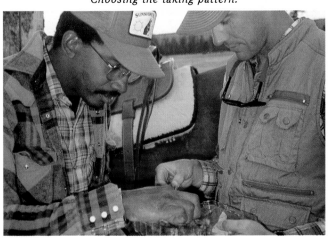

previous in sun drenched warmth mellowed by the contents of a wineskin. Now reality was cold rain trickling down one's neck. True, the memories of the large powerful cutthroat were fresh in our minds, but the snowflakes in the air as we ascended Heart Lake Geyser Basin added concern for the tedious six mile walk remaining. When we reached Paycheck Pass, snow was plastering trees and slushing the ground. No thoughts of ice cream sundaes or brewed perfections here! Now it was the warmth of our vehicle heaters and dry clothes. After these fantasies would come those of steaming mugs of coffee and a hot dinner at Flagg Ranch. The point of this tale is that Yellowstone's weather can change in an instant any time of the year. If you venture into its back country, be prepared.

Fall River Drainage

The drainage furthest west of the Continental Divide in Yellowstone National Park is that of Fall River, a major tributary to the Henry's Fork of the Snake River. Its drainage is adjacent to no major highway, thus its streams and lakes make for wilderness angling. Fall River's drainage borders those of the Firehole and the Madison rivers across the Continental Divide. The four major streams in the drainage (Bechler and Fall rivers, Boundary and Mountain Ash creek) begin on the Madison and Pitchstone plateaus and carve canyons across Cascade Corner which hosts the highest concentration of waterfalls in the Park. Below, each stream slows in Fall River Basin as if pondering the remaining journey. Then in the southwest corner of the Basin, they unite for the passage into Idaho and on to the Henry's

Twenty-six inch rainbow being released in Rocky Ford area.

◆

Fork. Technically not part of Fall River Basin, Robinson Creek also drains the Madison Plateau to the west of Boundary Creek and flows into Warm River in Idaho.

Like the Lewis River above its canyon and the Madison River drainage above Firehole Falls and Gibbon Falls, much of Fall River drainage was devoid of trout until recently. Quite possibly, but unproven, Cave Falls just inside the Park and Sheep Falls just outside may have been the historic upstream barriers for salmonids. No official records exist of nineteenth century planting, yet trout, apparently cutthroat, were found in Basin waters in a 1919 survey, and after that Yellowstone cutthroat were officially planted. Rainbow trout were unofficially introduced later, probably before the early 1930s. Both official and unofficial introductions to Fall River Basin have resulted in a powerful and hardy hybrid trout superficially identical to that which flourishes in the Henry's Fork drainage. This wonderful hybrid dominates the Basin waters below Cascade Corner where high waterfalls block its upstream progress. Above the falls the Yellowstone cutthroat reigns supreme, and none of the Basin waters contain mountain whitefish, suckers or chubs.

Bechler River and Boundary Creek

Bechler River is contained entirely within the Park, and is without major development. Bechler's beauty begins where the Gregg, Phillips, Littles and Ferris forks converge near Three Rivers Junction between the Madison and Pitchstone plateaus. Only the Gregg has a trout population. At Three Rivers Junction, thermal water adds nutrients and energy to alter the river for good trout habitation. This addition differs from in the Firehole River across the Continental Divide where the surface water conditions are overwhelmed by thermal inflows. Below the Three Rivers area are five miles through Bechler Canyon of rough and tumble waters, beautiful to behold but relatively inhospitable for trout. The angling season in the canyon begins around the first of July in normal runoff years when giant and

golden stoneflies emerge. Few anglers venture to the canyon this time of year, because of excellent angling on more approachable waters. By August and September, however, many persons including anglers pass along the trail in the canyon .

The canyon reach of Bechler River that is the most appealing to the fly fisher is below Colonnade Falls, the unique double falls marking the upstream egress of rainbow trout. Without a doubt, the most exciting time to fish the water from the Falls down to the mouth of Bechler Canyon and into the timbered end of the meadow is during the early July stonefly emergence. All fish in the canyon waters will first respond to large stonefly nymphs, then to large dry patterns fished to simulate egg laying adults. They will also bring responses from trout in the beaver ponds of Ouzel Creek below the 225 foot drop of spectacular Ouzel Falls. Soon after the stonefly emergence in Bechler Canyon, and from all waters of easing gradient in Fall River Basin, another important emergence occurs in canyon and timbered reach of meadow below Colonnade Falls. This is the brown drake emergence, and it is the most prolific in the basin, possibly excepting that of the pale morning dun (Ephemerella infrequens). This early and mid-July emergence is mainly an evening affair that begins in the silty gravels of the lower canyon and timbered meadow reach.

Perhaps the most notable reach of Bechler River, and its major tributary Boundary Creek, is that through Bechler Meadows. Fishing here can be difficult to the utmost because of the lack of overhead cover. This has inspired my friend and fellow angler Buck Goodrich to call this reach "graduate school for fly fishers". "Bring all your skills and first try all the other similar reaches in the Park, then come here to see how good you are!" says Buck, a veteran of thirty years of Fall River Basin angling. For about twenty years Buck and I have been humbled and seen each other enjoy spectacular days of angling in the meadows. The meadows have also been the site of some historical disputes. In the late nineteenth century stockmen unlawfully trailed herds of cattle here. To see the meadows is to understand why any stockman would covet them. Nevertheless because this occupancy was illegal, U.S. Army cavalry units sta-

◆

Boundary Creek in July.

Wild flower bloom in Bechler Meadows.

◆

tioned near Bechler Ranger Station skirmished with stockmen until the herds were removed early in this century.

In about two decades the next threat came to Fall River Basin in the need for storing irrigation water for agriculture on the Snake River Plain to the southwest in Idaho. Water users identified Bechler Meadows as a site for an irrigation reservoir with the dam placed downstream at Rocky Ford. On to the U.S. Congress they went declaring that the meadows were just mosquito infested moose pastures. Mistakes in surveys, they claimed, left it in the Park and, after all, the livelihood of farmers depended on the reservoir. The result would have been an impoundment of thousands of acres but of little more than a dozen feet in depth. In addition, because of the high runoff nature of Bechler River and Boundary Creek which would feed it, the reservoir would begin silting in immediately. Add to this the high surface area to volume ratio allowing huge evaporation losses, and the resulting reservoir would have been a useless ecological disaster. Environmentalists valued the area and fought to save the meadows. These groups protested to Congress and won. The result is that a unique and matchless quality fishery was preserved. Water users also won. Grassy Lake Dam, just outside of the park formed a deeper and therefore better reservoir. In the 1970s promoters in eastern Idaho proposed extending the Cave Falls Road on through the Basin, over the plateaus to connect with the Old Faithful–West Thumb Highway. The idea was ludicrous and the Park Service rejected it out of hand. In the 1930s one could drive an automobile from Bechler Ranger Station via the Bechler Meadows Trail to Boundary Creek on the west edge of the meadows. Like the road to the top of Paycheck Pass overlooking Heart Lake this was also closed. Over the years bag limit reductions and terminal gear restrictions have been applied to reduce angling impacts. The change in the 1980s to catch and release regulations for cutthroat and rainbow trout and grayling has given blanket protection to the entire fishery in Fall River Basin,

excepting recently added brook trout.

In Bechler Meadows the angling season begins with the ebb of runoff waters. The first resident aquatic insect of importance to emerge here is the pale morning dun. This event heralds the beginning of dry fly fishing in the meadow, and the incursion of windborne giant and golden stoneflies from the canyons above and below comes next. After this in the meadows comes the almost combined brown drake and green drake emergences. The mid-season here begins near the end of July when other than *Callibaetis* and a thin continuing *Baetis,* emergence all others diminish markedly from Bechler and Boundary creeks. Now, however, the terrestrial insect season begins throughout the Basin. Hoppers, beetles and ants are the main fare as waters recede and the meadows dry, but now more than ever "graduate school is in session" with clear waters and brilliant sunshine. Water temperatures at this time can also range up to the mid-sixties in degrees Fahrenheit, so in addition to increased wariness, trout are not as active as in the early season. By mid-September the autumn aquatic insect emergence takes place in Fall River Basin. The most important mayfly types making up this event are *Tricorythodes*, mahogany duns (*Paraleptophlebia species*) and gray drakes (*Siphlonurus occidentalis*). The best mahogany dun emergences are in the Rocky Ford area, while gray drakes and *Tricorythodes* emerge throughout. Another important emergence that occurs at this time from Basin waters is that of the great orange sedge (*Dicosmoecus atripes*), and like the gray drake and mahogany dun its appearance is during midday hours. Hoppers, of course, remain very numerous in the meadows, so the angler has a wide variety of insect types to present. The autumn emergence

◆

Trail signs at Bechler Ranger Station.

Cascade Creek near confluence with Fall River.

◆

can last into October, and typically intense feeding activity lasts for hours followed by dormant periods lasting for days.

The days of the late season can be the most enjoyable in Fall River Basin. Insect pests are gone, and so are most of the anglers. The usually clear air of mid-September to mid-October is ideal for photography and temperatures are optimal for activity during daytime. The angler will encounter more sightseers, photographers and backpackers this time of year. In fact, in many of my trips to Bechler River and Boundary Creek this time of year I do not begin fishing until midday. Morning finds me absorbed in photography. After this, it is on to the stream to catch the mahogany dun emergence, then it is out through the golden meadows with a ready camera to catch elk in the rut, moose or migrating waterfowl.

Bechler Ranger Station is the hub for starting most excursions into the west end of Fall River Basin. The station is almost exactly on the Idaho–Wyoming border and is accessed by a short road going north from the Cave Falls Road. From here the angler can begin day hikes, backpacking trips and trips with pack animals. The resident rangers have up–to–date information on trail conditions, water levels and campsite availability. They also have angling permits that must be in the possession of anglers within the Park. From the Ranger Station one can go by trail due east to Bechler River and upstream to Rocky Ford, northeast to Bechler Meadows and on up Bechler Canyon to either Old Faithful or Shoshone Lake, or north to Boundary Creek and up its canyon or northwest to Robinson Creek over the West Boundary Trail. One can also go due east on the South Boundary Trail to the east side of Fall River Basin. Other

than the access from Bechler Ranger Station one can access the west side of Fall River Basin from Cave Falls, the terminus of the only road in Fall River Basin in the Park. From here, as from the Ranger Station, one can access the east end of the Basin, but as we will soon see there are much better choices.

Fall River and Mountain Ash Creek

About a mile south of Ashton, Idaho an almost insignificant looking county road runs east from U.S. Highway 20. This is the Ashton–Flagg Ranch Road, also known as the Grassy Lake Road, and for the angler seeking a Yellowstone Park angling experience it is as important as any road within the Park. The Ashton–Flagg Ranch Road, still mostly unimproved gravel, came into being in the 1930s when Grassy Lake Dam was built just south of the Park boundary. This deep and cool reservoir, as we will see, influences the makeup of trout in Fall River below, and the road, which ends on the John D. Rockefeller Memorial Highway between Yellowstone and Grand Teton National Parks, provides access to Fall River.

The tributaries that form Fall River drain the southeast edge of the Pitchstone Plateau west of the Continental Divide. Like other waters in the Basin, isolation from man, superb water quality, good cover and food supply result in excellent numbers of trout. Near the east end of Fall River Basin, Beula Lake and its nearby twin, Hering Lake, have an important influence on Fall River. These two lakes, separated by a slough which dries up almost completely after the early season, moderate water temperatures for the immediate downstream waters of Fall River. Both lakes host only Yellowstone cutthroat

◆

Fall River Basin holds Yellowstone's best moose population.

Bechler River at Rocky Ford in October.

*Looking west down Fall River meadows with
Fish Lake in left foreground.*

trout. Beula offers more consistent angling and is more hospitable to trout. At just over 100 acres it is almost twice the size of Hering, and it has a continuous turnover of water with Fall River flowing into its southeast corner and out of its northwest corner. Fish of trophy size from Beula became increasingly rare up to twenty years ago because of a legal bag limit. In 1979 all waters in Fall River Basin over 7,200 feet in elevation were placed under a catch and release regulation. So an upswing in size of trout landed from Beula has taken place for better than a decade. Beula and Hering lakes, which are at 7,400 feet in elevation, represent a change of pace from the miles of streams in Fall River Basin. In the early season, which begins around the end of June, both lakes are best fished with leech and baitfish imitations. The most interesting angling here begins not much later with the damselfly emergence from both lakes, then the almost season long speckled dun emergence. In July one can stand on the inlet delta to Beula Lake and drift adult imitations of these into the lake. This tactic will bring good responses and will do the same later in the season with dry terrestrial and caddis patterns.

Some of the heaviest snow falls in Yellowstone National Park occur within Fall River Basin, so springtime warmth determines the point in time of the opening. Thus, early season access to Beula Lake is governed by the opening of Ashton–Flagg Ranch Road. The trail to Beula and Hering Lake, the most easterly access in the Basin, leaves this road and is an easy three mile walk, very suitable for backpacking with and without a float tube. In the same area one can access Grassy Lake Reservoir at several places as well as Fall River just inside the Park boundary. Below the Grassy Creek–Fall River confluence rainbow trout join the Fall River inhabitants. Just upstream of this point is the unnamed waterfall which prevents rainbow trout from entering the river and lakes above. Below this point Fall River drops into a photogenic canyon which holds mainly smallish trout. Back on the Ashton–Flagg Ranch

Road, however, there is access to good fishing just outside the Park. The outlet of Lake of the Woods combines with Cascade Creek and flows through a brushy meadow bordered on the north by the Ashton– Flagg Ranch Road. Here also is a good population of rainbow trout which migrate downstream to Fall River. Within the Park, just north of the Ashton–Flagg Ranch Road, one can walk down Cascade Creek to Terraced Falls on Fall River and experience a population of colorful hybrid trout. All this occurs in a dense pine forest which mostly escaped the devastating forest fires of 1988. In fact, the only area of Fall River Basin affected by these fires is the extreme eastern end near and above Beula Lake. About two miles west of Cascade Creek the South Boundary Trail leaves the Ashton–Flagg Ranch Road and drops down Calf Creek. Within two and a half miles the trail skirts the meadows along Fall River below its canyon. This access, however, is only convenient to the upper end of the meadow reach of Fall River and pales in attraction to the next one to the west off the Ashton–Flagg Ranch Road. This is the Fish Lake Road, and it provides the best access to not only Fall River, but Mountain Ash Creek and Proposition Creek.

Travelling west on the Ashton–Flagg Ranch Road from the highlands between the Grand Teton Range and Yellowstone National Park's Pitchstone Plateau a geographic transition occurs. Gone is the solid pine forest which envelops Beula Lake, Grassy Lake Reservoir, Lake of the Woods and the above mentioned streams. This new landform is Winegar Hole, a quiltwork of lilypad lakes, marshes, meadows, pine and quaking aspen groves. None of the surface water features here are impressive, but each contributes to the volume of Fall River. Water in the lakes and marshes is a remnant of huge blocks of ice that melted after the last ice age. Small streams emanating from the Teton Range course the Hole to end in Fall River. Some, such as Boone, Squirrel, and Conant hold good populations of cutthroat and brook trout, but Fall River is the major

Purple camas and buttercups in Fall River meadows.

Union Falls, 260 feet high, on Mountain Ash Creek.

A prime Fall River cutthroat-rainbow hybrid.

◆

attraction, and the Fish Lake Road is its gateway. Until 1987 the road ended at its namesake, then Winegar Hole Wilderness area was created on the extreme southwestern edge of Yellowstone National Park. Now the Fish Lake Road ends about a mile south of Fish Lake, so Fall River is a walk of slightly more than a mile from the new trailhead.

Fall River in its meadow reach and lower Mountain Ash Creek produce large trout. These consist of cutthroat, rainbow trout and their hybrids, but in the past few decades brook trout have reached these waters. This is because the State of Wyoming Game and Fish Department releases them in Fish Lake where they grow to trophy sizes. Brook trout from the lake escape early in the year via its intermittent outlet to Fall River. Occasionally they grow to trophy sizes downstream in Fall River and Mountain Ash Creek, but they are essentially a threat to increased cutthroat trout populations. But this most hospitable reach of river also receives a steady recruitment of cutthroat, rainbow and hybrid trout from instream spawning activities and from downstream drift from such water as Beula Lake, Lake of the Woods and Grassy Lake Reservoir. So trout are plentiful in the deep undercuts and pools. With respect to access, the South Boundary Trail does the same for the meadows along Fall River that the Bechler Meadows Trail does for Bechler River. The physical makeup of the meadow reach of Fall River, however, is somewhat different than that along Bechler River. Willows are much thicker here and beaver activity makes these meadows difficult to negotiate in places. All this means that there is more overhead cover for trout here than in streams in Bechler Meadows. There is very little inflow

of thermal water to Fall River throughout its reach while Bechler River receives a bigger share, not only in the Three Rivers area, but also at the upper end of Bechler Meadows. Another difference between the two streams is that Fall River experiences some inflow from Grassy Lake Reservoir during the agricultural irrigation season on the Snake River Plain. This inflow is governed by weather and so is unpredictable.

All streams in Fall River Basin are runoff courses, Fall River included. Thus the early season beginning varies, but usually can be relied on by the first week of July. The first significant aquatic insect to emerge is the pale morning dun. The next significant emergence, as in the rest of the Basin, is that of the giant and golden stoneflies. This emergence advances upstream through July and is important even in the meadow reaches because of wind. Another aquatic insect emerges throughout the Basin at this time. This is the mosquito, and during July it can be a pest of major proportions. But for the angler willing to tolerate mosquitos the rewards of angling on Fall River are unforgettable. As the large stonefly emergence dwindles those of the green and brown drake occur. Throughout Basin waters the green drake emergence is relatively short lived, lasting about a week in duration. Compare this to the green drake emergence from the richer waters of the Henry's Fork to the west. The occurrence in time of this emergence from the Henry's Fork is less variable than that in Fall River Basin for two major reasons. First the Henry's Fork is not a runoff stream of the same magnitude as are Fall River Basin streams and second the proximity of Island Park Reservoir moderates daily temperature fluctuations in waters flowing through Harriman State

Cave Falls: gateway to Fall River Basin.

◆

Park. As July progresses to a conclusion, terrestrial insects become a dominant food form for trout. Likewise the host of mosquitos diminish, but throughout the basin another terrestrial pest, the horsefly, emerges. These, of course, are nowhere near as numerous as mosquitos, but their bite is ferocious and distracting.

As July comes to a close another important emergence occurs throughout Fall River Basin. This is the berry season, and the most important of these are the low bush blueberries and huckleberries. The angler passing such areas as the South Boundary Trail west of the Fish Lake area or the Bechler River Trail east of the Ranger Station will encounter rich patches of these berries. For any visitor it will be difficult to refrain from collecting handfuls of these aromatic, luscious berries. Why put you through a discourse on berry picking when the subject of this book is angling? For the good reason that the berries attract bears, black and grizzly, to areas frequented by anglers. Fall River Basin holds one of the highest concentrations of black bears in the greater Yellowstone ecosystem, so it is not unusual to see these animals. Grizzly bears do not inhabit Fall River Basin in great numbers simply because there are no more than about four hundred in the entire ecosystem. They migrate to Fall River Basin during the berry season, thus it is possible to pass a patch and startle a harvesting bear. This can be a dangerous situation, particularly if cubs are present, so beware! All veteran Fall River Basin anglers have stories of bear encounters and subsequent actions. So take care in this angler's paradise, and here's hoping that your bear encounter will only result in an exciting addition to one of your angling tales!

When one goes west a few hundred yards on the South Boundary Trail from the Fish Lake access, a trail branching to the north is encountered. This is the Fall River Cutoff which crosses the namesake river and leads to Mountain Ash Creek, certainly one of the most beautiful and unforgettable trout streams in Yellowstone National Park. Within its low gradient downstream reaches are trophy sized cutthroat, rainbow and hybrid trout, and within its upper reaches are small colorful trout, picturesque canyons, cascades and one of the most

unusual waterfalls in the Rocky Mountains. This is Union Falls, formed by the confluence of two branches of Mountain Ash Creek. At 260 feet in height it is the second highest major falls in Yellowstone National Park. Mountain Ash Creek also brings one close to the history of the area. Early in the century the Marysville Road included the Cave Falls Road, went east past Bechler Ranger Station, across Rocky Ford, then Mountain Ash Creek and Proposition Creek. From here it went southeast to the Park boundary at the present Grassy Lake, then on to the Snake River. It was used to haul construction materials by ox and mule teams from the railroad at Marysville in Idaho to the Jackson Lake Dam site. One of the teamsters on the road in those days was Jack Dempsey, a future world heavy weight boxing champion.

The late season on Fall River and Mountain Ash Creek is mid-September to mid-October. Here, as in Bechler River and Boundary Creek one will experience a blanket *Tricorythodes* emergence and a good mahogany dun emergence. Trout will key on the latter, and it is most enjoyable to address those emergences with a lightweight system. In any case, the mahogany dun emergence can be found at its best in Fall River along those riffly reaches where the meadows pinch down. It is equally good throughout lower Mountain Ash Creek. Gray drakes emerge in best numbers in Fall River's meadow reaches, but the great orange sedge can be found throughout slower waters of both streams. Terrestrial insects, mainly hoppers, moths, beatles and ants continue in good numbers until about mid-October. By this time, however, one must expect changes in the weather that put down all surface angling. True, this can happen as early as mid-September throughout the Basin, but by mid-October the angler will see more days than not without fish feeding on the surface. So at this time what appears to work best in the early season works once again, and why not, water temperatures again never get higher than the mid-forty

◆

Trumpeter swans on Grebe Lake.

degree Fahrenheit range. At this time I have experienced early blizzards that cut short my day either by putting down fish or threatening to make trails and the tracks of unpaved roads difficult for passage. So by mid-October it may be time to leave Fall River Basin and its superb fisheries so as to not to risk being stranded with unpleasant consequences.

Madison River Drainage

Which is the most heralded drainage from a fly fishing standpoint in Yellowstone National Park? Undoubtedly the second largest in terms of surface area, that of the Madison River. More books, articles and videos are devoted to this drainage than any other in the Park, and for decades roads have almost entirely paralleled the Madison, Firehole and Gibbon Rivers. Also, many smaller quality trout streams of the drainage; Nez Perce, Duck, Maple, Little Firehole and Iron Spring creeks are easily approached. Charlie Brooks, the Bard of the Madison drainage, heralds its quality and accessibility best in his wonderful books. But whereas the angler may be crowded on the larger waters of the drainage, that person finds solitude on the smaller. The Madison River drainage offers more miles of easily accessible waters and a longer season than other Park waters (its waters have been restricted to only fly fishing since 1951). These pluses result in the highest number of annual visitations (except for Yellowstone Lake and River) since the beginning of the twentieth century.

Gibbon River and the Grayling Lakes

The Gibbon River, the second major source of the Madison River begins as small headwater streams feeding Grebe Lake. Both Grebe and Wolf lakes (and adjacent Cascade Lake) contain the only sustaining grayling population in the Park. Rainbow trout are also present in Grebe and Wolf lakes. Grebe Lake is an easy four mile walk from a trailhead on the Norris Canyon highway. Wolf Lake is most easily reached by walking to the Howard Eaton trail on the north side of the Grebe Lake outlet and proceeding about two miles west. Both grayling and rainbows are introduced, as are all salmonids above Gibbon Falls. Grayling were taken from Madison River stocks in 1921, and because of serious habitat degradation throughout their range, the Grayling Lakes serve as their refuge. But this is peculiar because grayling prefer running water. They, however, use suitable inlet and outlet streams here for their June spawning run.

Grayling are primarily insect feeders, so they are most active when damsel flies, midges, caddisflies and mayflies emerge from the lakes. Float tubing during these emergences is effective as is casting dry aquatic or terrestrial patterns from the shoreline in the evening. Rainbow trout, also introduced, flourish in Wolf and Grebe lakes. They can reach trophy sizes here, and are fished for not only in the same manner as for grayling, but also by presenting large streamer and leech patterns.

Below Wolf Lake, the Gibbon River drops into a narrow

canyon, then into Virginia Meadows where its gradient slows. This meadows reach is populated with small brook trout and rainbow and grayling escapees from the lakes above. Charlie Brooks, in his absorbing books, "The Living River" and "Fishing Yellowstone Waters", recommends that wet soft hackle patterns and small dry attractors are best for the angler here and in the Norris Meadows reach below Virginia Cascade.

Into the Norris Meadows area above Solfatara Creek the Gibbon is a relatively infertile stream. But in Norris Geyser Basin the Gibbon, like the Firehole in Lone Star Geyser area, gets a major contribution of geothermal water. This water increases both the dissolved nutrients and the water temperature of the stream, both making it, also like the Firehole, more hospitable. Geothermal waters supplying the Gibbon, however, are slightly acidic whereas those supplying the Firehole are slightly alkaline. Thus, the number of insect forms in the Gibbon is greater than that in the Firehole, but conversely and typically, the density of organisms is less in the Gibbon than in the Firehole. Plant life in the Gibbon also becomes richer below Norris Geyser Basin and brown trout make their first upstream appearance. Outstanding fishing is first realized in Elk Park, the meadows just below the cascades of the Gibbon exiting Norris Geyser Basin. Here are deep pools, undercut banks and aquatic vegetation. The successful angler is one with a practiced approach. Casts should be made not over the stream, and one's shadow should never fall on the stream. I have had my best success in Elk Park and in downstream Gibbon Meadows by drifting dry terrestrial and caddis patterns downstream, ahead of my position. Both Elk Park and Gibbon Meadows are adjacent to the Norris–Madison Junction highway, and are rich in wildlife that sometimes impede angling. Also just as likely, are disturbances from tourists or photographers seeking a better view of wildlife.

Below Gibbon Meadows the river drops into Gibbon

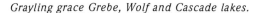

Grayling grace Grebe, Wolf and Cascade lakes.

Yellow wyethia near a 1988 forest fire burn area.

canyon which is closely paralleled by the Norris–Madison Junction road. Downstream is Gibbon Falls, the 80 foot high barrier to trout populations in the past. Good angling is present in the pools, riffles and runs. Below where the river heads into National Park Meadows, in which the meandering Gibbon and Firehole meet to form the Madison, the most interesting angling begins. As one would expect, large trout are present, but so are anglers as one of the larger campgrounds in the Park and Madison Junction, a major highway intersection, are nearby. Nevertheless success can usually be found here if one concentrates angling in the evening hours.

Thus the Gibbon is a series of meadows separated by reaches of fast water which are leaner in trout than the meadows. Caddisflies predominate throughout, while stoneflies are rare. Mayflies are present in the Gibbon with *Epeorus* species in the swifter reaches and blue winged olive, Siplonurus and Ephemerella species in the meadow reaches. Dragon and damselflies also populate meadow reaches, and I have found that early in the season patterns simulating their nymphs, particularly my beadhead peacock leech, are most effective. Of course, from late July into September, as on all Park streams, terrestrial patterns are excellent choices.

The Firehole River

The Firehole, the major source of the Madison River, begins in bogs atop the Madison Plateau. Technically the Firehole, because of being the major source, is really the Madison River. But what a loss that change would be to the world of rivers, for the name "Firehole" indicates a unique and singularly beautiful river.

Viewing the Firehole from almost any location, one concludes that this must be the epitome of trout streams. Most fly fishers (only fly fishing is allowed on the Firehole), however, find it difficult to accept that the trout population in the river above Firehole Falls is about one hundred years old! As on many of the Park's streams, barriers like Firehole Falls prevented the upstream spread of modern trout populations. So it was

Bull elk in January seeking heat at cliff base.

just disappeared.

It is not until the Firehole reaches the top of Biscuit Basin (the reach from the highway bridge upstream of Old Faithful down to the highway bridge above Biscuit Basin is closed to fishing to protect thermal features) that it becomes a heralded fishery. Here geothermal water inflow has massive positive (but also some negative) effects, like nowhere else on earth, on the trout population. In this reach of the Firehole to its canyon, mean winter water temperatures are in the low 50 degrees Fahrenheit, optimum for trout growth. Thus the growing season is surprisingly long with limits coming in the summer because of high water temperatures which forces trout into cool tributaries such as Iron Spring and Sentinel creeks. In addition to heating, geothermal water makes the river slightly alkaline and relatively rich in sodium chloride. This confuses many outdoor writers who label the Firehole a chalk stream. It is not. Chalk streams are rich in calcium bicarbonate coming from the dissolution of limestone or lime (calcium carbonate) containing rocks and subsequent hydration.

Disturbingly many veteran Firehole anglers observe that the river has warmed significantly since a series of earthquakes in 1970. The most notable of these is Charlie Brooks. With alarm and some frustration he discusses this phenomena in "Fishing Yellowstone Waters" and "The Living River". He and others also observe that the average size of trout landed appears to have decreased since that time.

From Biscuit Basin down to its canyon the Firehole River is a series of meadow reaches interspersed by riffle and run water. Below the riffle downstream of Biscuit Basin begins the most fabled reach of the Firehole, that flowing through Midway

that in 1889 brook trout were introduced into the Firehole River. However, the Firehole below Upper Geyser Basin proved too warm for brook trout, so they either perished or fled to cooler reaches above or into tributaries. In 1890 the more adaptive brown trout were introduced into Nez Perce Creek. Now they flourish in the Firehole. In 1922, rainbow trout were introduced into the Little Firehole River. They too flourished, but the choicest lies throughout are usually inhabited by large, aggressive browns. As with the introduction of trout in other barren Park waters, there has been some folly in the Firehole drainage. Yellow perch stocked in drainage ponds, including Goose Lake, were finally eradicated in 1938. Black bass stocked in many of these places, and the Gibbon River as well,

Muleshoe Bend, Firehole River.

Time to move to the next hole.

◆

and Lower Geyser basins. The first excellent water is the tight loop that Charlie Brooks dubbed Muleshoe Bend. The next is the reach of water, named again by Charlie, Goose Lake Meadows. This area hosts Goose Lake which holds rainbow trout, but being so fond of running water, I have never fished it. I spend more time in the picturesque waters below the Lower Iron Bridge, known as Ojo Caliente Bend. It is an excellent place to fish particularly in the spring before the river is too warm for the trout to be active. Near the top of the bend Fairy Creek enters, and about halfway through the bend Sentinel Creek enters, each from the west. I consider these streams to be sanctuaries for heat stressed trout, thus I avoid them in the summer, but I return to this area in September to present terrestrial insect imitations in the river.

Below Ojo Caliente Bend the Fountain Flats reach is an early season nymphing favorite because of the presence of damsel and dragon fly nymphs. Also, stonefly adult patterns drifted on the waters here can be effective in the spring. The reason is that winds blow these insects up from the canyon. I have received scorn and chuckles from anglers who notice my terminal gear this time of year on the Firehole. No doubt these skeptics would not scorn the trout I have encountered through use of these patterns.

In days gone by this area had a human population. The Fountain Flats Hotel was just north of the Fountain geyser group. It operated from 1881 to 1904 and housed 350 guests. It was a social center with steam heat, running water and electricity, but it came to disuse when the Old Faithful Inn was built. Also, just east of the Nez Perce Creek confluence soldier stations existed until near the turn of the century. Now there are only a few picnic areas along the river.

When you view the Firehole River, consider that trout here are a gift, and that quality is subject to geologic instability. How many times has the Firehole experienced geologic warming and cooling? We know not. Was there a past trout population here? Thus the Firehole remains a sweet mystery. Mystery adds enjoyment of speculation to angling, and for the optimist the return of numerous large trout to the Firehole is just

around the corner. For the pessimist they never should have been there in the first place. Whatever your outlook, the Firehole is there to enjoy. If you have not fished it you miss an angling experience. If you have, you love it.

The Madison River

The native salomnids of the Madison River were west slope cutthroat trout, whitefish and Montana grayling. By the 1930s these were replaced by the downstream drift of rainbows and browns from the Firehole and Gibbon. To many anglers these were more desirable sport fish, so little protest resulted. Brown trout were even stocked in the Madison in 1929, and in the 1930s both rainbow and grayling were planted. Of the original native salmonids only the hardy mountain whitefish remains. Occasionally brook trout and grayling are caught in the Park reach. It appears that a few cutthroat reside here, but grayling are definitely downstream migrants from Wolf and Grebe lakes. The same is true of brook trout which migrate from both the Firehole and Gibbon rivers.

The Madison River begins at the confluence of the Gibbon and Firehole rivers just southwest of Madison Junction, fourteen miles inside the Park's west entrance. Only minor geothermal water addition occurs along its reach, so flowing westerly it cools and becomes consistent. This moderation makes it an excellent trout stream. Gone are the stressing influences of geothermal waters, so trout behavior in the Madison is more conventional than in the Firehole or Gibbon.

Brown trout, native and from Hebgen Lake, spawn in the autumn in the upper reaches of the Madison. Many progeny remain in the river, while others gradually descend to Hebgen Lake. Rainbow trout parallel these actions with a spring run out of Hebgen and an autumn run at about the same time as the brown run. Like the browns, the spawners migrate back down

◆

Buffalo near Madison River.

Bull elk in Madison River Meadows

◆

to the lake and their progeny follow later. The result of native and migrant usage is an excellent trout population.

In a chemical sense the Madison River, like its sources, is a sodium bicarbonate–sodium chloride stream. But like the Firehole it has been misnamed a limestone stream because of appearance. The Madison River in the Park and its major tributaries flow through volcanic rhyolitic and tuff formations. These contain silicate compounds which release their sodium content more easily than their calcium content, and therein lies the difference. Physical factors make the Madison a great fishery. Within the Park its gradient averages a few tenths of a percent. The mean annual temperature of the Madison is 50 degrees Fahrenheit. Generous cover and ideal substrate are present. The result is that the Madison is one of the most hospitable streams on earth for salmonids.

Within Yellowstone National Park the Madison River is primarily a meadow stream punctuated by riffle and run stretches. The upper meadow reach begins at the confluence in National Park Meadows. It ends almost two miles downstream at what Charlie Brooks called Big Bend. Below, to where the river swings northwest and leaves the highway, are a series of meadow stretches and riffle–run areas. This section of the Madison sees the most angling pressure, as can be guessed by the number of pullouts and because of Madison Junction Campground just below its beginning. This is a worthy reach, but from mid-June to Labor Day it is occupied by anglers and tourists from all over the world. You will be questioned in all languages and crowded by those having just as much right to be here as you. You will also encounter wildlife along the

meadows within the Madison Canyon. Most numerous, of course, are waterfowl. Magnificent bison, moose and elk also reside here. Each year visitors are gored or trampled because of coming too close to these. If these animals block your route, give way and return later. You are the intruder.

If you fish the meadows of the Madison in the early season, wet flies are best. In my experience, dragon and damselfly nymph imitations are a must. Smaller attractor nymphs, especially bead heads, are also effective. As the waters warm with

◆

Rainbow returning to the Madison River.

advancing spring, aquatic insects (and anglers) emerge here. These include caddis and pale morning dun and green drake mayflies, but the most fabled time to fish the meadow reaches along the west entrance highway is during the summer terrestrial season. At this time a variety of hopper, ant and beetle patterns are a must. So is a stealthy approach.

Below Seven Mile Bridge the Madison changes to a riffle and run stream for miles. Here is the famous Grasshopper Bank, named for obvious reasons. This area is the last spot along the highway adjacent to the river, and its prime is from the end of July through September. You bet it is frequented then by hopeful anglers. Beyond is the Long Riffle, which marks the parting of road and river, and downstream is perhaps the most famous reach of the Madison in the Park. This is "The Barns" area named after horses, coaches and buses that were corralled or stored in the past for transporting Park tourists. From Cable Car Run down about three miles to the Beaver Meadows is a series of deep runs. The upstream end of this reach is accessed almost directly from a gravel road going north from the west entrance highway just east of the west entrance. This area is primarily stonefly water, dominated in mass by the giant stonefly, *Pteronarcys californica*. Any large nymph pattern will produce when presented properly. When adult stoneflies are flying or dropping eggs onto the surface here, presenting large dry flies can result in some of the best top water fishing around.

By late September brown and rainbow trout migrate upstream from Hebgen Lake just west of the Park. These fish seem to regard the deep runs of The Barns area as resting spots before proceeding upstream, so large colorful streamers will bring strikes, particularly on overcast days. On bright days these fish seem to respond only at daybreak and twilight. As Bud Lilly emphasizes in his "Guide to Western Fly Fishing", this autumn migration results in the best fishing here and those big fish picture from this site most probably were taken during the event.

Below The Barnes area is the last reach of the Madison River in the Park. This is the Beaver Meadows, the section requiring the most effort to reach. You can walk downstream from The Barns area to access these meadows, or you can access them from Baker's Hole Campground or Highway 191 north of West Yellowstone. From any access the Beaver Meadows gives you to the best of the Madison River, an unspoiled meadow holding almost three miles of river with no more development than angler trails. Fishing this paradise is not difficult. Starting in the spring you can attract browns and rainbows with dragonfly and damsel nymph imitations fished deep. So a sink tip line and a short, stout leader are just as vital here as in deep swift runs. As the season advances to mid-June, aquatic insect activity improves. Pale morning dun mayflies, caddisflies and a sparse green drake emergence occurs. For the dry fly fisher the real attraction to the Beaver Meadows begins about mid-July, the start of terrestrial season. Hoppers are the main fare and presentation is much more important than pattern selection. Long floats are a must, and come to think of it, the more you have your fly off the water, the fewer fish you will catch. This season in the Beaver Meadows lasts well into September and overlaps the spawning run of brown and rainbow trout out of Hebgen Reservoir. These fish pass through the Beaver Meadows with good energy reserves, so encounters with them are thrilling. The most exciting way to enjoy them has been, for me, with a hair mouse. I present these with best

◆

Trail to the Beaver Meadows in October.

A Beaver Meadows Brown.

Woolly Bugger

Polar-Aire Minnow

Woolly Worm

JJ Special

White Marabou Muddler

Hornberg

Beadhead Peacock Leech

Beadhead Goldenstone Nymph

Brook's Montana Stone

March Brown Nymph

Gem State (Green Drake) Nymph

Brook's Little Gray Caddis

Beadhead PT Nymph

PT Nymph

Terminator

Zug Bug

Sandy Mite

Gold Ribbed Hare's Ear

Partridge and Yellow Soft Hackle

Partridge and Brown Soft Hackle

PMD Emerger

Sofa Pillow

Park's Stonefly

Dry Muddler

Matt's Golden Stone

Jay-Dave's Hopper

Joe's Hopper

Trude

Blond Humpy

Royal Wulff

Adams

Light Variant

Green Drake Muddle-May

H+L Variant

Dry Spruce Fly

Parachute Gray Drake

Brown Drake

No Hackle Dun

Sparkle Dun

Goddard Caddis

CDC Hemmingway Caddis

Elk Hair Caddis

Antron Caddis

Spent Partridge Caddis

Deer Hair Spider

Cinnamon Ant

Foam Beetle

U-Con 2

Duck Creek in early June.

results in the evening hours when trout are willing to come to the surface. Admittedly I do not take many trout with this tactic, but when I do exhilaration from their volcanic strike compensates. One definite problem with this tactic is the resultant late exit from the meadows. This makes a reliable flashlight a must, but over the years I have punctured waders and lost equipment. The standard way of attracting large migrating browns and rainbows works better in the Beaver Meadows. This technique consists of presenting large streamers deep into runs or along undercut banks. Again, almost any such pattern will be effective if presented correctly.

Hebgen Lake Tributaries

Just north of the Madison River at Baker's Hole are Maple, Duck and Grayling creeks which begin in the Park and end in the Grayling Arm of Hebgen Reservoir. Before Hebgen Dam was built, they combined in the marshes north of Horse Butte and flowed westerly to meet the Madison further down the valley. Each of these streams offers attractive angling.

Is Cougar Creek really Maple Creek, or is it just the opposite? Most sources say Cougar Creek ends in sink holes within the Park and so is as secretive as its namesake. Thus, what one sees when travelling north on Highway 191 out of West Yellowstone is really Maple Creek, not the signed Cougar Creek. Take your pick, the purpose of this book is not to name geographic features, or pick sides. In any case this creek flowing out of the Park to meet Duck Creek a bit to the west holds some excellent beaver ponds with brown and rainbow trout up

to trophy sizes, but they are wary as any on earth. In the creek that ends in sinks to the east (your choice, Maple or Cougar), is an isolated and rarely fished population of west slope cutthroat trout.

Duck Creek is formed almost two miles inside the Park by the combination of Richards Creek from the south, Gneiss Creek from the east and Campanula Creek from the north. Its nearly three mile length within the Park is a superb but difficult meadow reach holding trophy brook, rainbow and brown trout. These fish are wary beyond belief, so for most anglers Duck Creek is frustrating. I have literally crawled on my hands and knees in late September to approach holes that I know contain large brown trout. Nevertheless, in the afternoon a perfectly drifted hopper pattern of your choice or a precisely placed leech pattern in the evening will bring out wary residents. Delicate caddis patterns may work anytime. The meadows along Duck Creek have recently been populated by buffalo from the Park's increasing herd. Keep their presence in mind. Campanula Creek holds trout only during spawning periods and most of Richards Creek and its source, Richards Pond, is presently off limits. This area is a critical grizzly bear migration route, so it is appropriate that it is little disturbed during studies of their passage. To the east of Duck Creek is a long reach of Gneiss Creek holding waters seldom fished. The brook, brown and rainbow trout here rival, in size, those in Duck Creek below, but they are not as wary.

As one travels Highway 191 past Duck Creek and the Highway 287 junction, the road ascends. Just before it passes back into the Park a beautiful stream crosses, then parallels on

36

the east. It parallels and crosses the road for miles, then disappears to the east. This is Grayling Creek, but only cutthroat trout are present. Will its namesake be restored here some day? Physically and chemically the waters are appropriate. No contemplative angler would complain of protective angling regulations or even a ban of angling here to reestablish the lovely endangered species. Let's see what the future holds!

Gallatin River Drainage

The streams that form the Gallatin River begin on Three Rivers Peak in the Gallatin Range, flow into Gallatin Lake, then down into a long sloping meadow. Here trout first populate the river. When one travels north on Highway 191 over the divide that separates Grayling Creek of the Madison River drainage from the Gallatin River drainage, fishless Divide Lake and its outlet are on the east. Then flowing from the southeast, the Gallatin River, no more than a fair sized creek, comes into view. About a half mile north, where Divide Creek meets the river, Big Horn Pass Trail leaves the highway to parallel the river. This trail is the access to the upper river, and by following it one can realize some excellent headwater angling, mainly for cutthroat trout.

Almost two miles downstream of the Big Horn Pass trailhead is another trail that also heads east. This is the Fawn Pass Trail, and through its use one can access meadow reaches on Fan Creek and its major tributary, Fawn Creek. Both these streams can be surprisingly exciting to fish, especially during the summer terrestrial season, and the waters flowing from these and from Bacon Rind Creek, flowing from the west, help make the Gallatin River a more interesting stream.

Below the Fan Creek confluence the Gallatin hosts more browns and rainbows than it does above. This combined with its increased size, good riffles and runs mean that it attracts more anglers than the reach above. Below the Fan Creek confluence the Gallatin is also perhaps the most accessible river in the Park. Thus it is common to find the highway pull outs along this reach filled with angler's vehicles much of the season. Caddis species predominate with a smattering of stone flies. Slate–cream duns and blue winged olive mayflies are also present. Browns and rainbows can range up to good sizes, and I find that they are most active during the terrestrial season. Essentially, the Park reach of the Gallatin is overshadowed by its waters in the canyon below. But for those who stop and test the waters here, the result is willing browns and rainbows with an occasional cutthroat responding from a stream flowing through beautiful surroundings.

Yellowstone River Drainage

The Yellowstone River drainage dominates Yellowstone National Park, and like the Snake River and Fall River drainages only a fraction is accessible by road. Easy access is only in the middle of the drainage. Nevertheless, Yellowstone River and Yellowstone Lake are respectively the second and first most popular fisheries in the Park. This drainage is overwhelmingly inhabited by the Yellowstone cutthroat trout, and it once may have been the sole domain of this species within the Park. The superlative "largest" not only applies to the lake and drainage, but also to the length of the river within the Park, the depth of first the Grand Canyon of the Yellowstone and second of Black Canyon. Grayling, whitefish and all species of trout present in

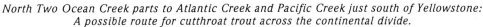

North Two Ocean Creek parts to Atlantic Creek and Pacific Creek just south of Yellowstone:
A possible route for cutthroat trout across the continental divide.

Photo by Rich Tillotson

Confluence of Yellowstone River and Thorofare Creek above Yellowstone Lake.

the Park are in the Yellowstone drainage. This includes the recent illegal introduction of lake trout in Yellowstone Lake. This presence alone is the only known exotic salmonid residing above lower Yellowstone Falls because brook trout appear to be recently eliminated from Arnica Creek, a tributary to the West Thumb of Yellowstone Lake.

The Yellowstone drainage was nearly the victim of some of the more ludicrous water usage schemes to be proposed for Yellowstone Park. During the 1920s, for example, it was proposed to divert Yellowstone Lake water by a tunnel across the Continental Divide to Shoshone Lake, thence by tunnel again to the Henry's Fork where the water could be used for irrigation projects in Idaho. An earlier, even more laughable, scheme was to harness Upper and Lower Yellowstone Falls to power an electric railway that would transport tourists and goods around the Park.

Upper Yellowstone River

Like its neighbor, the Snake River, the Yellowstone River has its sources south of the Park. From here it flows north from the Absaroka Range through the flat plain that was once the bed of a larger prehistoric Yellowstone Lake. The Absaroka Range borders the river to the east forming the Park boundary. To the west is the Two Ocean Plateau, down which runs the Continental Divide separating the Yellowstone and Snake River drainages and over which colonizing cutthroats from the Snake River appeared to have crossed millennia ago to evolve into

present day Yellowstone cutthroat trout.

Below Bridger Lake the river is joined by Thorofare Creek, its largest tributary above the lake, then a succession of streams laden with snow melt into July. This inflow combined with the mainly silt bottom of the old lake bed limits the food forms thus limiting the number of resident trout. The few anglers that visit this reach in early summer see a paradise of streams apparently filled with cutthroat ranging to trophy sizes. But these fish are returnees to the lake after spawning, and they ravenously strike

Yellowstone Lake from Lake Butte.

A sincere message at Pelican Creek trailhead.

almost any fly offered. They make great sport into September, but by October only a remnant is present. The main attraction here is unforgettable scenery and abundant wildlife as one travels the reach. So the river above the lake serves best as an unspoiled avenue to conduct the Yellowstone cutthroat each spring to pristine spawning grounds in tributaries and to conduct resultant recruits down to the lake. It must also be revered as the pathway by which cutthroat originally moved to inhabit the entire Yellowstone River drainage.

Yellowstone Lake

This is the Park's major natural feature, yet today it is just a remnant of its self in glacial times. What it has evolved into is the host of the largest inland cutthroat trout population in the world. This alone makes it invaluable, and the presence of its trout population has almost been its undoing. When man first encroached on the Park, the cutthroat trout population of the lake seemed endless. Nothing, it was thought, could threaten it and so began incredible neglect. First, commercial fishing to supply eateries within the Park and nearby communities was established. Tourists wasted thousands of fish. Hatchery operations in the first half of the twentieth century extracted several hundred million cutthroat trout eggs from spawning fish in the lake and its tributaries. These facts make the present excellent fishing conditions in the lake somewhat of a miracle. Continuous angling restrictions since the 1960s, when it was a distinct possibility that the lake's unique fishery could be lost, have saved it from a more rapid demise.

Yellowstone Lake does not produce abundant food for trout because of the insoluble country rock and almost alpine climate. Most food forms for trout are concentrated in the warmer shallow waters. Crustaceans dominate, and midges are the most important aquatic insect. Leeches and small quantities of mayflies and caddisflies are present. Thus trout here feed in shallow water, and this fact dictates safe angling strategy. Yellowstone Lake, you see, can turn from glassy morning calm to a raging expanse of four foot whitecaps within an hour of wind. Stand on its north shoreline when the wind picks up.

You will gain quick respect for the danger of being on the lake. Talk to someone who has capsized a watercraft on the lake, or read the accounts of how many souls have died over the years on its stormy surface. Consider all this and the habits of mature trout in the lake and you will see that the shallows, whether you wade or use a float tube, offer the best angling on Yellowstone Lake. This holds true whether you fish adjacent to the highways or venture to the beautiful, remote arms of the lake. Leech and fresh water shrimp patterns always seem to work on the lake. My favorite locations are the sandbars along West Thumb and Bridge Bay. In particular, these spots are enjoyable on calm summer mornings and evenings. Emerging midges and speckled duns can result in non-stop action from cruising cutthroat. Insulated waders to help one get about waist deep are enough to reach the action.

A reason for improved cutthroat trout populations in Yellowstone Lake is the closing of spawning tributaries to fishing until mid-July. Two creeks, Clear and Cub, hold major spawning runs, an important food source for black and grizzly bears. These streams draining into the northeast corner of Yellowstone Lake are closed to angling until mid-August, so both bears and trout benefit. Just to the north and west of these two streams is Pelican Creek, the lake's second largest tributary. The lower two miles of this creek are closed to angling to protect migratory waterfowl, but above the closure superb angling for the cutthroat returnees to the lake can be had for a week or two after the mid-July opening. Fortunately, Yellowstone Lake abounds in tributaries useful to spawning cutthroat trout, and whether it be Bridge Creek, Arnica Creek, Beaverdam Creek, Chipmunk Creek or Grouse Creek, each has its run. Some, like Trail Creek, adjacent to the upper Yellowstone River, host lakes. Alder Lake is a few hundred yards up an outlet on the peninsula that separates the south and southeast arms of the lake. Just off West Thumb, almost on

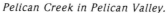

Pelican Creek in Pelican Valley.

the Continental Divide, sits Riddle Lake and its outlet Solution Creek. These lakes and others hold fishable cutthroat populations.

A further example of past mistakes here was the introduction of Atlantic salmon and rainbow trout in Yellowstone Lake. Angler-introduced lake chubs appear to be rare. What is worrisome, however, is the recent illegal planting of lake trout. In the summer of 1994 juveniles were caught for the first time. The transplant is dangerous to the cutthroat trout population and the wildlife that depends on it for food. Mature cutthroat trout tend to inhabit shallow water, and lake trout inhabit the depths. But mature lake trout prey on juvenile cutthroat which also reside in deeper water. Heavy preying could bring a decrease in cutthroat in the lake. If so, mammals and birds depending on them would be cheated of a prime food source. Park fisheries managers are tasked with locating lake trout spawning sites and to identify possible eradication methods. Law enforcement officials are working to determine the perpetrators of this act and to develop measures to prevent its reoccurrence. It is true that in hospitable Heart Lake, just over the Continental Divide, cutthroat trout and lake trout coexist in good numbers. But what is at stake in Yellowstone Lake is the world's greatest inland cutthroat population. In addition, the potential is present for diminishing this population to the point that all life forms depending on it will likewise diminish. The resultant loss would have a major negative impact on the quality of Yellowstone National Park.

Yellowstone River

Below Yellowstone Lake the river is an almost ideal trout stream. Nearly half of this reach, however, is closed to angling to protect wildlife or fragile landforms. Not only does this reach encompass all water types, it is also the most approachable portion of the river within the Park. The Canyon–Fishing Bridge highway is never more than a mile from its banks making the reach the best known and most heralded of the rivers within the Park. Cutthroat trout are its sole salmonid, and these remain in a spawning mode until early summer. The lake above

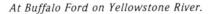

At Buffalo Ford on Yellowstone River.

Photo by Ken Retallic

Close encounters at Buffalo Ford

moderates water temperatures, reduces silt, and dampens extremes in water flows. It also supplies a downstream drift that enriches the food base.

Usually just after the river between the lake and waterfalls opens to angling, green drakes and caddisflies emerge. Soon after, gray drakes, flavs, *Callibaetis* and tricos, emerge in succession. By mid-summer successful angling requires identifying which emerging insect trout are keying on. Charlie Brooks in his "Fishing Yellowstone Waters" talks of fifty and even seventy fish days in the reach, with fish up to three pounds. Now, because of more restrictive regulations, fish to five pounds are possible. Anglers at Buffalo Ford experience these fish, and because one can literally drive to the river, it is one of the most popular of all angling locations. Here riffles and runs are the dominant features, and because no large obstacles break the current, trout commonly come to the feet of anglers to find respite. I once told a non–angling friend of as many as six trout at my feet. She didn't believe me. When I offered to take her there to observe, she asked why I thought she would go anywhere with someone telling such a story. If one wants solitude at Buffalo Ford, the best chance to find it is in October. By this time, however, tiny midge emergences take over. It's a beautiful and invigorating time of year, but old man winter is just around the corner. Below the Alum Creek closure to the Upper Falls the river changes in character. Writers such as Brooks and Dave Hughes describe how the current tugs one's feet downstream. The river here is less hospitable to trout than the reach above the closure. Nevertheless, good numbers of fish are present.

Essentially, the Lower Falls marks the downstream end of exclusively cutthroat trout water in the Yellowstone River. It also marks the last easily approachable water until the Tower Falls area near the end of the Grand Canyon. Only Broad Creek can be considered a major tributary to the river in the Grand Canyon reach, and it also is a cutthroat trout domain. Near Tower Falls, walk–in anglers can usually enjoy good action, but the best comes with the upstream passage of the giant and golden stonefly emergences sometime in the second half of

Lower Falls of the Yellowstone River.

◆

July. Tower Creek itself is worth fishing for rainbow trout above its picturesque falls. Below the Tower Junction–Roosevelt area the river leaves the Grand Canyon and is easily approached from the bridge on the northeast entrance highway. Not far below, the Lamar River enters near the head of the Black Canyon. Increasingly, rainbow trout dominate going downstream into the Black Canyon, and brown trout become important below Knowles Falls.

Without a doubt the most popular destination in upper Black Canyon is the Hellroaring Creek area. A shortcut from the gravel pit just north of Floating Island Lake makes the walk to the river a bit more than a mile. Downstream, the next practical route to the river is from the Blacktail Creek trailhead where a four mile walk is required. Like the site above, a suspension bridge allows one to cross the river. These waters are open to angling in mid-June, but because the Yellowstone is a major runoff stream, good conditions usually are not found until later. When the waters clear and lower, the large stonefly emergences bring spectacular responses by trout. In the canyon, this emergence can be expected during the last two weeks of July.

After the stonefly emergence passes, a lull seems to overtake the fishing in Black Canyon until September. At this time the changing of seasons triggers trout to caddis and terrestrial insects. A large, brightly-colored hopper presented along overhangs and grassy banks is almost sure to bring midday hits well into October. Large streamers fished in runs also bring results,

but in October winter clashes with autumn, so gauge the weather if a walk of several miles is required to reach a canyon location.

Lamar River Drainage

In the lower part of its reach through the Park the Yellowstone River is joined by two important rivers. The furthest upstream, the Lamar, is the larger. Like the Snake River, on the other side of the Park, it flows through upstream formations which erode to cloud its waters during persistent rains. This condition can last for a few days and even hampers angling in the Yellowstone River below. Like the Snake River, angling on the Lamar diminishes in quality as one goes upstream from the reach adjacent to the highway. Nevertheless, there are good numbers of small cutthroat in the upper river. If an angler desires solitude in beautiful surroundings, the upper Lamar or its tributaries are excellent locations. For combining beauty and good angling Cache, Calfee and Miller creeks are best. Anglers enjoy naming landmarks, and the Lamar confluence with Soda Butte Creek is christened the Junction Pool. This landmark, just off the northeast entrance highway, marks the upstream point of best angling on the Lamar. Below are about twelve miles of river, almost evenly divided between beautiful meadows and the lower canyon reach.

When the Lamar normally clears of runoff in late June, large stoneflies emerge from the canyon waters. First, one should present nymph imitations, and it is wise to carry these regardless of the season. Then the real fun starts in canyon waters as floating stonefly patterns bring hard strikes from cutthroat, rainbows and their hybrids. The cutthroat are native, and rainbows were released in the 1930s and may also have entered from the Yellowstone River. After the stonefly emergence, caddisflies are the main aquatic event that attract trout. These are joined in mid-summer by terrestrial insects.

Regardless of the season, the angler who tests the canyon waters will see that some rock scrambling is required to approach the canyon, but its nearness to the highway mini-

◆

*Grand Canyon of the Yellowstone River
below Inspiration Point.*

Yellowstone River at Calcite Hot Springs and Bumpus Butte.

mizes time required in doing this. The proximity to the meadow reach above also means that two types of waters can easily be fished in a day on the Lamar, and one is an alternative if the trout in the other are not in a cooperative mood.

Whereas the canyon reach of the Lamar has more forgiving waters with respect to presentation, the meadow reach above is the opposite. Here presentation is everything because the sky is the backdrop. Mayflies are relatively sparse here because of the silt load. Caddis are abundant. Like no other stream I have experienced, activity seems to be scattered on this reach. In a hundred yards of river fish will be quite active, then one can walk for maybe a quarter of a mile over what appears to be fine water before another active pod of fish are found.

Over the years the Park buffalo herd has increased to over four thousand animals. One place where this increase seems obvious is the Lamar Valley, so observe your surroundings. These powerful beasts damage more people in Yellowstone Park each year than any other animal, including bears. Lamar Valley is also a best location to observe timber wolves reintroduced to Yellowstone in 1995.

As with all meadow reaches in late summer and early autumn, terrestrial patterns work well, and streamer patterns become more effective. But again beware of the weather at this time of year. The Roosevelt Junction–Cooke City highway is one of the most isolated in the Park, and snow squalls that slicken the roads at this time of year can turn the trip to town into a headache.

Soda Butte Creek is the third largest tributary to the Lamar River. This fine stream coursing from the northeast has been the focus of concern in recent years because a proposed gold mining project in its watershed, just outside the Park, threatens its water quality. Past mining operations have impacted the Soda Butte Creek fishery, but the effects have diminished with time. The current threat, however, is bigger because of the proposed scale, so a battle rages between those who protect the Park and surrounding ecosystem and those who wish to profit from minerals adjacent to it. Soda Butte Creek is also one of the Park's most popular fisheries. The best trout are concentrated below Icebox Canyon because of increased water from Pebble Creek and Amphitheater Creek, both of which offer good fishing for smaller trout. Caddisflies are the predominant aquatic

Mountain sheep near Mount Washburn.

42

insect, but as summer progresses the grasses of adjacent meadows host abundant terrestrial insects.

About a mile below the Pebble Creek confluence with Soda Butte Creek is a small parking area on the north side of the highway. From here a trail of just over a half mile leads to Trout Lake. Trout Lake always contained large fish and was formerly called Fish Lake by nearby residents who used these fish as table fare and spared no means to capture them. Until 1950, this lake was also a major fish hatchery for producing cutthroat trout eggs and later those of rainbow trout. To function as such its size was increased to twelve acres by damming its outlet. The lake still holds some of the largest cutthroat–rainbow hybrids in the Park. These fish replenish their numbers by spawning in the inlet stream. During its season, which begins in mid-June, Trout Lake can be fished from the bank or by float tube. If you fish from a float tube, remember that the Park requires a boat permit and a life preserver. Rest assured that the ranger attending the inlet creek will check for these items. One day a leech pattern produces, the next day it is flashback nymphs to simulate scuds, then for days on end nothing produces well. Damselflies and speckled duns will produce sporadically, but the lure of trout to double figure poundage brings anglers well into October.

About fifteen stream miles downstream from the Soda Butte Creek confluence the most visited stream in the drainage enters the Lamar River. This is Slough Creek, and it has attained an international reputation. I first fished Slough Creek in the mid-1970s, and only in the meadow below Slough Creek campground did I see many anglers. Now it is common to see dozens of vehicles parked along the benches overlooking that meadow and at the trailhead to the upper meadows. Between these meadows, and for a mile above its confluence with the Lamar, are relatively short reaches of swifter waters. The one major barrier between these meadows is the cascade about a mile above the campground at the head of the lowest meadow. Above it, the only salmonid present is the Yellowstone cutthroat trout. Below it rainbow trout are also present. The origin of rainbow trout in Slough Creek is not as clear as for cutthroat. They may have entered from early stockings in Buffalo Creek, a

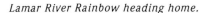

Lamar River Rainbow heading home.

Grand Canyon of the Yellowstone near Northeast Highway Crossing.

tributary which enters near the campground, while cutthroat were always present in abundance. Part of the reason for that knowledge is that the present day Silvertip Ranch predates the Park and provided a means for angling. Passage rights to this private property remain in the form of the tote road beginning just below the campground, proceeding up the ridge, then paralleling the meadows along Slough Creek. It is common to see wagons or pack trains, loaded with gear and visitors, moving along the road.

The meadow below Slough Creek Campground holds about three miles of intriguing stream down to the so–called VIP Pool. On clear, windless mornings, throughout this reach, one can see immense trout holding on the bottom of pools. Many succumbed before the 1970s when subsistence anglers flocked to the reach. Slough Creek now is open only to catch and release fly fishing, and vehicle access to the lower meadow is prohibited, so these large trout face a better future. It is still permissible to park along the benches above this reach. This means that numerous anglers are encountered here between the beginning of the season and the end sometime in October. In early July I have had success on the lower end of the meadow drifting stonefly adult imitations into the larger holes. Pale morning duns also produce at these times, as do humpies and irresistibles because of the scattered evening emergence of brown drakes. After that time, hopper patterns produce into September. If you prefer wet flies, leeches, damselfly and dragonfly nymph patterns work best, but the real fun is drifting the dries down through riffles to the holes below. By September one would expect terrestrials to be the main fare for trout here. Not so! Green drakes which normally emerge elsewhere in the early season provide trout with an abundant food form. Gray drakes also emerge in September, so large mayfly patterns usually produce well in this reach. As this reach approaches the upstream campground, it changes to a pool and riffle stream which also contains good fish.

Just below the campground, and across from the corral which serves the Silvertip Ranch, is a trailhead with parking space. For anglers the tote road that begins here is a stairway to heaven. After an invigorating walk through the pine forest and quaking aspen groves, one emerges in a meadow of absolute beauty. Deep water with cruising cutthroat trout is literally at one's feet. Upstream in the tall grass meadow is the trace of more bends. To the right are picturesque patrol cabins sited decades ago for combating poachers. This is the "first meadow above", meaning the first meadow above the campground. The gradient is gentle, and the cover abundant. Insect life is plentiful because Slough Creek, in terms of essential dissolved nutrients, is one of the richest streams in the Park. This is because it runs mostly through relatively soluble sedimentary rocks. Mayflies, caddisflies, midges, craneflies, damselflies and dragonflies emerge from the meadow reaches. From the riffles and runs that punctuate these, stoneflies and more caddisflies emerge. Pale morning duns are the dominant early season mayflies. By the midseason speckled duns dominate. These give way to autumn green drakes, but caddis species remain numerous throughout the season. As with all meadow reaches, hoppers from midseason to autumn offer exciting angling. Ant swarms can also bring exciting fishing in each meadow when late summer rolls around. The first meadow above holds as much stream as the meadow below the campground, but cutthroats here are less wary than their hybridized cousins below. They do not match the hybrids in size, but fish exceeding three pounds are present. At the upper end of the meadow there is an old bridge abutment. If one crosses just below here, heads northwest and up the bench another beautiful site awaits. This is McBride Lake, named for Jim McBride an early Park scout and chief ranger. The lake is less than a half mile walk from Slough Creek, so a midday side trip offers not only an angling change of scene, but a spectacular photographic subject.

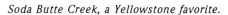

Soda Butte Creek, a Yellowstone favorite.

Trout Lake.

If the "first meadow above" is an angler's paradise, then the second meadow above the campground is beyond superlative. This meadow, two miles beyond the first meadow above, is the largest meadow reach on Slough Creek. It extends north of the Park, and throughout it the creek meanders through deep holes. Abundant cutthroat trout range up to two feet in length here. Emerging insects are the same as in the meadows below and angling strategies that work in those places apply. Take time to observe this special place when you test its waters. You will never forget the "second meadow above", a special destination in the world of angling.

Gardner River Drainage

The last major downstream tributary to the Yellowstone River in the Park is the Gardner River. It is almost like two rivers. Above Osprey Falls the drainage hosts mostly small brook trout and rainbow trout, both introduced early in this century. The streams above Osprey Falls are the only waters in the Park open to bait fishing. This is restricted to children up to age twelve. Trout here respond well to any small fly, so for one who enjoys small streams, the area is a delight.

Below Osprey Falls the Gardner River passes through a steep canyon not hospitable to fishing. In the Mammoth–Tower Junction area crossing it becomes friendlier and brown and rainbow trout are plentiful. The most abundant aquatic insect is the giant stonefly which emerges by early July. Thus at this time the choice of what to fish with is obvious. If one prefers small dry flies on the lower river, adult caddis patterns through-

Second meadow above the campground, Slough Creek.

◆

out the season and hoppers from midsummer to the first of October are the best choices.

Beginning in mid-September, the event which makes the Gardner most attractive occurs. This is the brown trout run from the Yellowstone River. Fish up to several pounds participate and in the fast, rocky water offer a strong challenge. Certain areas of the river are closed at this time of year to protect spawning, but in opened areas the angler can test his skills. Large brown are frequently hooked, but not frequently landed. Charlie Brooks, again in "Fishing Yellowstone Waters", speaks of anglers cleaned by hooked browns careening back to the Yellowstone River. The luckless souls are left with broken leaders and feelings as empty as their reels. I know the feeling, but the one or two good fish landed makes an autumn trip to the Gardner a memorable experience.

On Forming an Angling Strategy for Yellowstone Park Waters

Creating a successful fly fishing strategy uses the conditioning of fish to feed in a manner that results in the most energy gained for the least energy expended. Trout feed on the most available nutritious food form or the largest food form. Thus, the mechanism for taking trout is to present flies which represent the organism they momentarily seek throughout the season. For trout waters it goes like this: Large wet flies (nymphs or streamers) are effective throughout the season on all Park waters. Their effectiveness, however, peaks twice: Early in the season and late in the season. Early in the season

rising water temperatures induce trout feeding activity. In addition, cutthroat and most rainbows have recently spawned, so they attempt to replenish used energy. At this time warming waters are too cool for massive insect emergences. Leeches, earthworms, dragonfly nymphs, stonefly nymphs, riffle beetle larva and baitfish are some of the large food forms that are available in the early season. Therefore, they are sought by foraging trout and the angler should present their imitations. True, most of these food forms are available throughout the season, but as time passes through the early season aquatic insects become more available. Thus, the angler should turn to presenting dry and wet simulations, not only of their various

◆

Bunsen Peak north of Gardner's Hole.

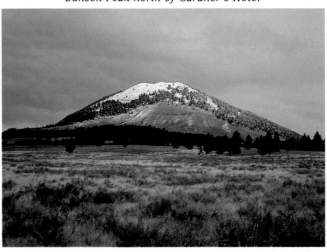

45

Bald Eagle.

◆

life stages, but simulations of the specific types that are most available at the time. These will be various species of caddisflies, damselflies, mayflies, stoneflies and others. As the early season aquatic insect emergence passes, terrestrial insect populations become increasingly available for trout. The angler must turn to presenting imitations of such insects as ants, beetles and hoppers into the late season when the lesser emergence of aquatic insects occurs. At this time the angler must determine which aquatic or terrestrial insect imitation is best suited for success, a situation similar to the early season aquatic insect emergence. As autumn passes, both aquatic and terrestrial activity lessen with the start of cold weather. Thus, the angler

turns to presenting large wet flies again.

What emerges is a cycle of presentations that produces successful angling, and beneath this cycle is the principle of energy conservation, the first law of thermodynamics. Like any fundamental law, however, implementation may not always be obvious. You can understand this caveat if you have been frustrated in finding the taking pattern in a multiple emergence situation. All the above dialogue applies to Yellowstone Park waters, and details would make a lengthy but interesting book. What I have given is a framework. To fill out that framework for Yellowstone Park waters, absorb as much as possible from the books I cited to create this issue.

Flies For Yellowstone Park Waters

Recommending flies is a subjective activity because of experience and perception differences. Collective experience is more valuable. This is because flies for a variety of situations would be identified, thus giving the inquiring angler information for any situation. I thus contacted several experienced Yellowstone Park anglers for recommendations that resulted in the selection given on the following plate. Some of these flies are new, others have been around for decades. The contributors whose experience also span decades include:

John Bailey, Livingston, Montana
Pat Barnes, Helena, Montana
Al Beatty, Bozeman, Montana
Gretchen Beatty, Bozeman, Montana

◆

May fly duns by the author.

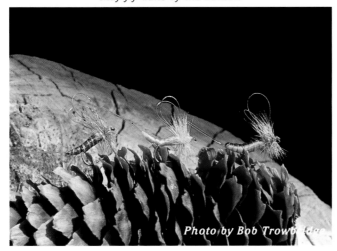

Bill Black, Roseburg, Oregon
Paul Bowen, Rexburg, Idaho
Jay Buchner, Jackson, Wyoming
Kathy Buchner, Jackson, Wyoming
Howard Cole, Jackson, Wyoming
Chuck Collins, Pocatello, Idaho
Jack Dennis, Jackson, Wyoming
Jim Gabettas, Idaho Falls, Idaho
Buck Goodrich, Shelley, Idaho
Rene Harrop, St. Anthony, Idaho
Bonnie Harrop, St. Anthony, Idaho
Bob Jacklin, West Yellowstone, Montana
James Jones, Jackson, Wyoming
John Juracek, West Yellowstone, Montana
Mike Lawson, St. Anthony, Idaho
Bud Lilly, Bozeman, Montana
Craig Mathews, West Yellowstone, Montana
Matt Minch, Gardiner, Montana
Ralph Moon, Chester, Idaho
Syl Nemes, Bozeman, Montana
Richard Parks, Gardiner, Montana
Jack Parker, Idaho Falls, Idaho
Harold Roberts, Idaho Falls, Idaho
Tim Tollett, Dillon, Montana
Tom Travis, Livingston, Montana
Bob Trowbridge, Providence, Utah
Tim Wade, Cody, Wyoming

Equipment Selection For Yellowstone Park Waters

Many anglers question my choice of a seven–weight system for presenting all flies in large and medium sizes on Yellowstone Park waters. My answer is a four letter word: "wind". Yellowstone's wind makes a nine foot rod of medium flex in this system near ideal when combined with weight forward lines of all types. I spend less time casting than with a six–weight system. Much more important is the fact that I can use a slightly heavier leader (up to 3X), allowing me to play fish more quickly thus preserving their energy. For presentation on smaller Park streams, or when only small flies take fish, I use a four–weight system. For larger waters I prefer nine foot rods in this system and seven footers in this system for small waters. I am also partial to weight forward lines for four–weight systems.

Not only can you depend on wind when angling in the Park, you can expect weather conditions from brilliant sunshine to violent blizzards and thundershowers. These can happen throughout the angling season, so bring clothing suitable for comfort in all conditions. Park waters are cold. Temperatures dipping to the thirties and forties in degrees Fahrenheit are common early and late in the season. Even hardy anglers will need insulated waders in these waters. During the midseason insulated waders are still a wise choice for the less hardy person, but there are July and August days with air temperatures in the seventies and eighties of degrees Fahrenheit when wading wet is comfortable.

A brimmed hat that protects ears and eyes is necessary in the brilliant high country sunshine. So are sunglasses, not only to help you in viewing the depths but also for protection from ultra–violet radiation. Another essential, regardless of your skin pigmentation, is a tube of sunblock with a skin protection factor of at least thirty.

Yellowstone Park is one of the natural wonders of our world. Take time to observe the surrounding countryside and include a camera to preserve your memories of this wonderland.

Bidding Farewell to a Sweet Fishing Season

I watched the season die in an amber sea of curing meadow grass and yellowing willows. Distant solitary quaking aspen quivered orange in the surrounding pine forests.

Through that amber sea I go to a last rendezvous with the river. Mallards and Canada geese wheel and glide to rest in the amber sea before the journeys of tomorrow. Snow forms a thin veneer on the shadowed side of the distant mountains. On adjacent plateaus, the forest monarch bugles an intent to conduct the rites of the ages. Above all is the transparent blue morning sky.

Now I have gained the river flowing over black and yellow gravels that formed the canyon ramparts and volcanic plateaus of yesteryear. In the green transparent flow of the river, shadows generated from submerged ledges and boulders swirl downstream. How quietly the river glides, relaxed and constant through the straight flats.

Below is a deep bend, silent and cold. Deliberately and carefully I approach it, and yes, in its depths are those fleeting shadows. Almost unseen, then silent and sinuous they glide over the gravels protected by the transparent green depths.

Back into the amber sea I slide to wait for the warmth of the advancing day. Wait there for that meager warmth to reach those shadows and for my eyes to absorb the surrounding symphony.

A soft "shuck" alerts me to the river's edge. Through the amber stalks I see concentric ellipses widening and softening on a downstream drift through the bend. "Shuck" comes another signal. Then "shuck" again, at the top of the bend as the fleeting shadows have risen to sip drifting glints of life in the early afternoon.

Deliberate and focused I arc to the flat just above the bend. Out onto the surface I settle my likeness of those drifting glints of life. Down it goes to the bend. A pulse quickens and thuds in my throat. Everything beyond that drifting fraud is a void.

"Shuck!" and I apply gentle pressure to feel the responding surge of power. Out of the water erupts the surprising silvery length, twisting, full–bodied and leaving suspended sparkling globules of water. Down to the safety of the depths it plunges to become the fleeting shadow again.

But the fraud holds tight and persistent pressure brings the shadow to the surface again. Up it twists to clear the surface by feet, then once again. Next comes the panicky headlong flight through the bend to the run below. Through the run it slices gaining distance on my persistent pressure. In the next bend downstream it erupts over the surface again. I approach the bend to regain control. But seeing me for the first time the trout bursts to the far bank and slices upstream to its home in the bend above.

I'm now below and in command. With persistent pressure I force the trout down into the run where with each attempt to regain its haven, it shows more and more colorful flanks and its creamy belly. Now strength to perform the deep borings and twisting jumps is gone. There are short thrusts and rolls to regain the deep water sanctuary and the security of being a fleeting shadow.

But more and more the thrusts and tugs are punctuated by time spent rolling onto its flanks. So with care I approach the gasping, twisting form. The last lunges for freedom are weak and open mouthed. But the beauty of her flanks now absorb me. I guide her by hand to the gravel bar. There, while on her side, I gently remove the fraud from her jaw. I cradle her back through calf–deep, icy water where the gentle life giving flow reflects sky and sunlight. She rolls there exhausted in my hands, her flanks shining first crimson and olive with grains of black, then silver and cream. What a perfection of symmetry and color she is!

Now she is reviving with slow sinuous turns in my hands. Her gill covers rise and fall with slow and rhythmic motion. She rights herself without my help as the cold gentle current breathes more life into her. I feel her steadily gain strength and stability in my hands. Slowly she exits my hold to descend to the depths of the hole.

Goodbye! Become the fleeting shadow again. May the waters of winter hold you undisturbed for months. May you grow and be wise for the rites of spring and our encounters next season. Goodbye, my friend.

Now the autumn sun glides low toward the distant ridges. The crystallizing air gently enriches the remaining colors. It speaks of winter's cold grip as vapors rise from the river and mark my own breath. I must go to return to life's responsibilities. So goodbye, my friend.

Goodbye, sweet season.

(First published in the Idaho Falls Post Register, November, 1991)

Bibliography

Brooks, Charles E., *Fishing Yellowstone Waters*, Winchester Press, 1984.

Haines, Aubrey L., *The Yellowstone Story: Volumes 1 and 2 Yellowstone National Park*. The Yellowstone Library and Museum Association, 1977.

Hughes, Dave, *The Yellowstone River and its Angling*, Frank Amato Publications, 1992.

Jones, R. D. et. al., "Fishery and Aquatic Management Program in Yellowstone National Park." U.S. Fish and Wildlife Service, Technical reports for the years 1980–1993, Yellowstone National Park, Wyoming.

Lilly, Bud and Paul Schullery, *Bud Lilly's Guide to Western Fly Fishing*, Lyons & Burford, 1987.

Mathews, Craig and John Juracek, *Fly Patterns of Yellowstone*, Blue Ribbon Flies, 1987.

Mathews, Craig and John Juracek, *Fishing Yellowstone Hatches*, Blue Ribbon Flies, 1992.

Pierce, Steve, *The Lakes of Yellowstone*, The Mountaineers, 1987.

Varley, John and Paul Schullery, *Freshwater Wilderness: Yellowstone Fishes and Their World*: Yellowstone National Park: The Yellowstone Library and Museum Association, 1983.

Too close for comfort.

Photo by Ken Retallic